© Anna Bryukhanova/iStockphoto.com

Enrichment Magazine

IN THIS ISSUE . . .

To the Director

This student folder contains nine study leaflets and the enrichment magazine. Remove the center staple and distribute the leaflets as indicated in the leaders guide. This magazine should be distributed at the first session for use throughout the course.

3558 S. Jefferson Ave., St. Louis, MO 63118-3968
1-800-325-3040 • www.cph.org

Written by Reed Lessing
Edited by Brian Chisamore

Cover illustration © CPH /Greg Copeland
Graphic design by Tamara Bishop

This publication may be available in braille, in large print, or on cassette tape for the visually impaired. Please allow 8 to 12 weeks for delivery. Write to Lutheran Blind Mission, 7550 Watson Rd., St. Louis, MO 63119-4409; call toll-free 1-888-215-2455; or visit the Web site: www.blindmission.org.

Manufactured in the United States of America

1 2 3 4 5 6 7 8 9 10 22 21 20 19 18 17 16 15 14 13

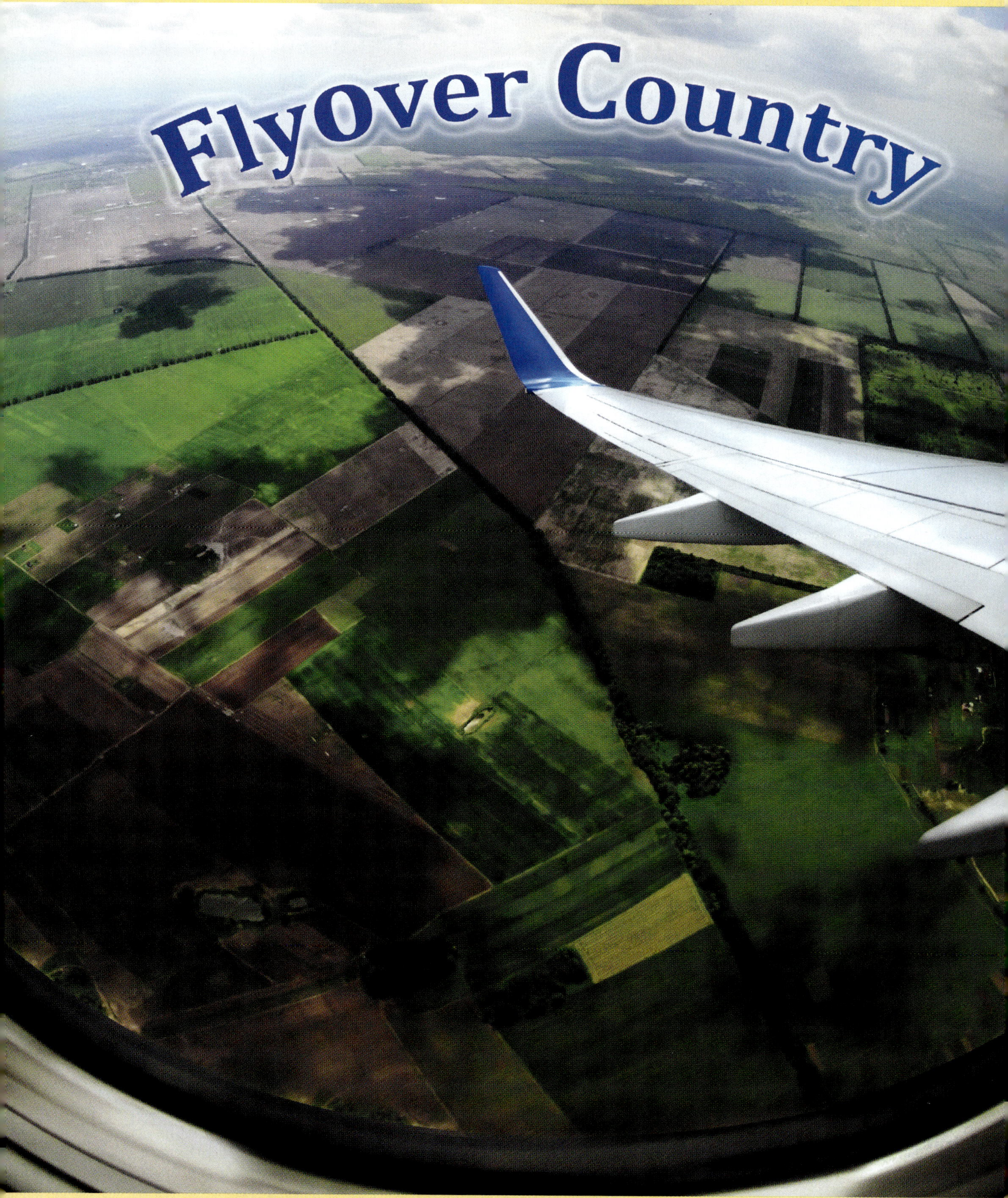
Flyover Country

There are parts of the United States that some people call "flyover country" because they don't see these areas as being very exciting. You have to fly over them to get to other more exotic places, like New York or LA. Without stepping on too many toes, I suggest that Iowa, Nebraska, and Kansas are the top three flyover states. And having served as a pastor in Broken Arrow, Oklahoma, for ten years, I must admit that the Sooner State is in the top ten.

There are portions of the Bible that are considered to be "flyover" books. Perhaps one of yours is Leviticus with all of its sacrifices or Numbers with all of its, well, numbers! First Chronicles is right up there on my list of "flyovers." It begins with nine chapters of genealogies.

And then for many people, there are Ezra and Nehemiah—flyovers, if ever there were any!

Slowing Down to Take a Look

No writings from the Old Testament historical books are more neglected, perhaps because they contain so many lengthy tabulations that include those who followed Cyrus's decree in 538 BC and traveled from Babylon to Jerusalem. The list also contains the number of their horses, mules, camels, and donkeys (Ezra 2; Nehemiah 7:6–73). But this is just the beginning. There is a listing of the family heads and those registered with them who came up with Ezra from Babylon during the reign of King Artaxerxes I in 458 BC (Ezra 8:1–14), priests who married foreign women (Ezra 10:18–44), people who helped rebuild the wall of Jerusalem (Nehemiah 3), Judahites who pledged their allegiance to the Lord (Nehemiah 10:1–27), provincial leaders who settled in Jerusalem (Nehemiah 11), and priests and Levites who returned with Zerubbabel (Nehemiah 12:1–37).

What is our collective response to all of these unknown names? *Fly over!*

But even as we fly over Ezra and Nehemiah at 35,000 feet, we can't help but glance out the window. Look! Down there! Do you see it? There are pieces of broken rubble, burned-out timber, and destruction everywhere.

Wreckage and ruin mark every chapter in Ezra and Nehemiah. Ezra is faced with a decimated temple, while Nehemiah must deal with crumpled walls. Sanballat asks with disdain if the people are able to "revive the stones out of the heaps of rubbish" (Nehemiah 4:2). The answer is twofold. No, they cannot. But, yes, God can! He empowers Ezra and Nehemiah to rebuild Jerusalem.

A bit more than half of the Book of Ezra is devoted to rebuilding the temple. Cyrus's decree concerns only the temple, so those who returned from Babylon did so "to rebuild the house of the Lord that is in Jerusalem" (Ezra 1:5).

Nehemiah's mandate, on the other hand, is to repair Jerusalem's walls and repopulate the city. God is committed to these walls, for they ensure Jerusalem's safety and independence. They are continually before Him (Isaiah 49:16). When Nehemiah orchestrates the rebuilding of the walls (according to Nehemiah 6:15, it took fifty-two days), it becomes an occasion for great rejoicing.

These two gifted leaders lived in Jerusalem from about

458 to 425 BC. Their work solidified God's people during the Persian period that began under Cyrus (539 BC) and ended with the military might of Alexander the Great (356–323 BC). Through Ezra and Nehemiah, the shattered remains from Babylon's destruction in 587 BC rose again!

It is just like our God to launch a great work with broken bricks and busted beams. After all, the barren Sarah gives birth to the son of promise (Genesis 21:1–3). Hebrew slaves inherit the land flowing with milk and honey (Joshua 1–12). A ruddy runt named David becomes a giant-killer (1 Samuel 17). And the stone the builders rejected has become the cornerstone (Psalm 118:22).

And this is all marvelous in our eyes!

Prophets in the eighth century BC who envisioned a rebuilt city include Amos (Amos 9:11–15) and Hosea (Hosea 3). But Isaiah is the chief proponent of a renewed Jerusalem. The city is a constant theme throughout the book. Days are coming when all nations will stream to it because the Lord will send forth His Torah from Jerusalem (Isaiah 2:3). Toward the end of Isaiah, the prophet increasingly describes the future grandeur of Jerusalem. In the age to come, it will be the center of the "new heavens and a new earth" (Isaiah 65:17–25).

Isaiah 54 beautifully describes the city's full splendor emerging from the ashes of exile. God says, "O afflicted one, storm-tossed and not comforted, behold, I will set your stones in antimony, and lay your foundations with sapphires. I will make your pinnacles of agate, your gates of carbuncles, and all your wall of precious stones" (vv. 11–12). The precious stones that adorn the refurbished city are like some of the high priest's jewels on his breastplate. Just imagine! In place of broken walls, stained with blood and smoke, the Lord is going to adorn them with black mortar that will highlight their beauty. Israel never added precious stones to Jerusalem's foundations and walls; doing so would have prompted enemy attack. This implies, then, that Isaiah is also describing a future city, where enemies will no longer threaten God's people.

These promises of a rebuilt city are also for us, because we know the pain of flyover lands. More often than we probably care to admit, you and I live in places that are desolate, dry, and dead, filled with tumbleweeds and blowing sand. In these ruins, wagging fingers and torching tongues remind us of our past sin. Desert demons live in these badlands, pointing out our ugly duplicity, ongoing pride, and lustful idolatry. Our plan becomes one of denial. We do anything but face our huge heartaches. The goal becomes singular. Fly over!

Landing the Plane

Ezra and Nehemiah know. O God, they know! All th pain of Babylon and all the torment of exile are captured i their books. But the same God who used them to rebuil Jerusalem is also rebuilding our lives. Our foundation is Jesu (1 Corinthians 3:11). His sacrificial death, glorious resurrection and gift of the Holy Spirit guarantee that we presently have ful citizenship in the new Jerusalem (Philippians 3:20).

But there is more building to come. God's promises i Ezra and Nehemiah are only partially fulfilled. They will reac their consummation when Christ comes again to usher us int the new Jerusalem, which will shine with everlasting glor (Revelation 21). And so it is time to put our seatbacks an tray tables in their upright position, turn off all our electroni devices, land our plane, get out, and look much more closel at the beautiful Books of Ezra and Nehemiah!

GETTING SOME BACKGROUND

The Books of Ezra and Nehemiah frequently mention Babylon. They assume we know how the Israelites ended up in the land of the Tigris and Euphrates Rivers.

What about you? Do you know the story?

Let's get some background!

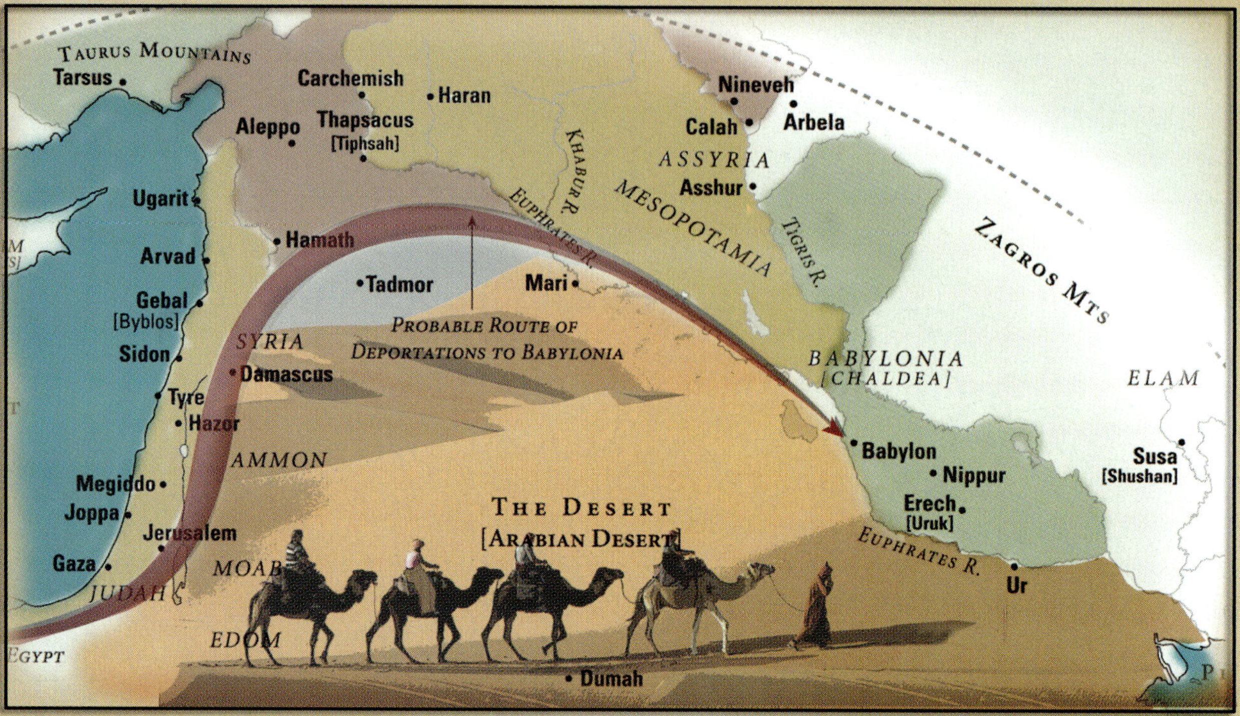

Dying a Slow Death

At one time, during the Davidic/Solomonic era in the ninth century BC, Israel was on top of the ancient Near Eastern world. The nation appeared to have everything. But the ironic twist is that these liberated slaves from Egypt began to enslave one another. The oppressed in Egypt became the oppressors in the Promised Land. They neglected the needs of the orphan, the widow, and the alien in the gate. Beginning with Solomon, Jerusalem became the new Egypt, and everything began to fall apart.

Psalm 106 reviews this slow death. Israel sinned, forgot, rebelled, craved wickedness, became jealous, worshiped other gods, despised the Promised Land, murmured, provoked the Lord to anger, mixed with the nations, sacrificed their children, and played the harlot. The final verdict was the Babylonian exile in 587 BC. This was God's means to enact his Sinaitic covenant curses (e.g., Leviticus 26; Deuteronomy 28), bring Israel to its senses, purge the nation of idolatry, and renew its mission to the world. Nebuzaradan, the commander of the Babylonian imperial guard, puts it this way: "The Lord your God pronounced this disaster against this place. The Lord has brought it about, and has done as He said. Because you sinned against the Lord and did not obey His voice, this thing has come upon you" (Jeremiah 40:2–3).

The Babylonian Empire was an alliance of two disparate peoples, the Medes in the Zagros Mountains to the east and the Chaldeans in southern Mesopotamia. The coalition overthrew the Assyrian Empire with its defeat of Nineveh in 612 BC. The dynasty's moment in the sun, however, was fleeting. It barely outlasted its greatest king, Nebuchadnezzar II. Babylon began with Nabopolassar's ascension to the throne in 626 BC and ended with the invasion of Cyrus the Great in 539 BC.

Enforced Deportations

The Babylonians inflicted four deportations on the people of Judah:

1. 605 BC, in the third year of Jehoiakim (Daniel 1:1–7)
2. 598 BC, during the reign of Jehoiachin (2 Kings 24:10–17)
3. 587 BC, during the rule of Zedekiah (2 Kings 25:1–21)
4. 582 BC (Jeremiah 52:30)

These exiles were a mammoth rupture in Israel's life.

Perspective on these Babylonian expulsions comes by considering how the Assyrians treated the countries they conquered. Assyria practiced cross-deportation because their goal was to establish economically productive provinces throughout the empire. On the other hand, the Babylonian program may be likened to "slash and burn." The demographic movement was one way—to the heartland of the empire. Babylonians did not invest time and effort in creating productive provinces. They engaged in military campaigns to secure tribute and to support construction in their urban centers.

Some Judeans who were carried away to Babylon were enlisted for work in the temple, while the Book of Ezekiel attests to another community that was more agrarian. These settlements were by the Chebar River. According to Jeremiah 29, many of the exiles enjoyed a degree of freedom in these refugee camps. They were allowed to build homes, cultivate fields, and engage in business. But, lest they get too comfortable there, both Jeremiah 24 and Ezekiel 37 indicate that God's plan is to bring them back to the Promised Land.

The distinction in the practice of exile by the two Mesopotamian empires, Assyria and Babylon, can be underscored by attention to the numbers of Israelites taken in their respective exiles. As for that of Samaria, the author of 2 Kings offers no comment about the number of Israelites taken, other than the statement that "the Lord rejected all the descendants of Israel" (17:20). Assyrian inscriptions offer greater detail. The so-called Sargon II display inscription reports: "I besieged and conquered Samaria. 27,290 people who lived in its midst, I carried away." Another text, the Sargon II Nimrud Prism, puts the figure at 27,280. On the other hand, according to Jeremiah 52:30, the total number of Babylonian deportees was 4,600. This probably denotes only men. Adding women and children brings the aggregate number to around 15,000. The bottom line is this: there is good reason to believe that far fewer people were taken into exile by the Babylonians than were taken by the Assyrians.

This much is also certain. Whatever the exact number was, the Babylonian exile left Jerusalem like a ghost town, with few people living in and around its precincts (e.g., 2 Kings 25; Jeremiah 40–43). After the fall of Samaria in 722 BC, the Assyrians brought newcomers into the land, and there was economic development. The Babylonians did not resettle people from other lands, so the population of Jerusalem and Judah remained small. After 587 BC, Israelite families were scattered, villagers lived in cities, the royal class had no palace, and priests had no altar. Everything was turned upside down and inside out.

Between the Iron Age (1200–550 BC) and the Persian period (520–333 BC), Jerusalem and her neighboring villages declined in population by 90 percent, while the land of Judah fell by 70 percent. This means that the region closest to Jerusalem suffered a mortal blow at the hand of the Babylonians. Those who were not killed in warfare were exiled, while those not exiled abandoned their homes and went somewhere—anywhere—for stability and civilization.

In God's Remembrance

Yet as terrible as the conquest of Judah was—as terrible as times were as each of the four waves of deportees were led away from Judah to Babylon—there one amazing fact about the Babylonian exile. There is one thing that makes this exile stand out as far different from that suffered by the Northern Kingdom under their Assyrian conquerors. The people of Judah were remembered by God.

In Psalm 106, we read that God "remembered His covenant, and relented according to the abundance of His steadfast love" (v. 45). God relented. In other words, the exile was not permanent. After a time, by God's grace, it came to an end. As we see in Ezra and Nehemiah, many of the descendants of those taken in exile were able to travel to, and settle in, Judah and Jerusalem. These people joyfully made the journey because of one very important reason: God had not forgotten them but had remembered them and the promises He made to them.

CYRUS:
GOD'S ANOINTED DELIVERER

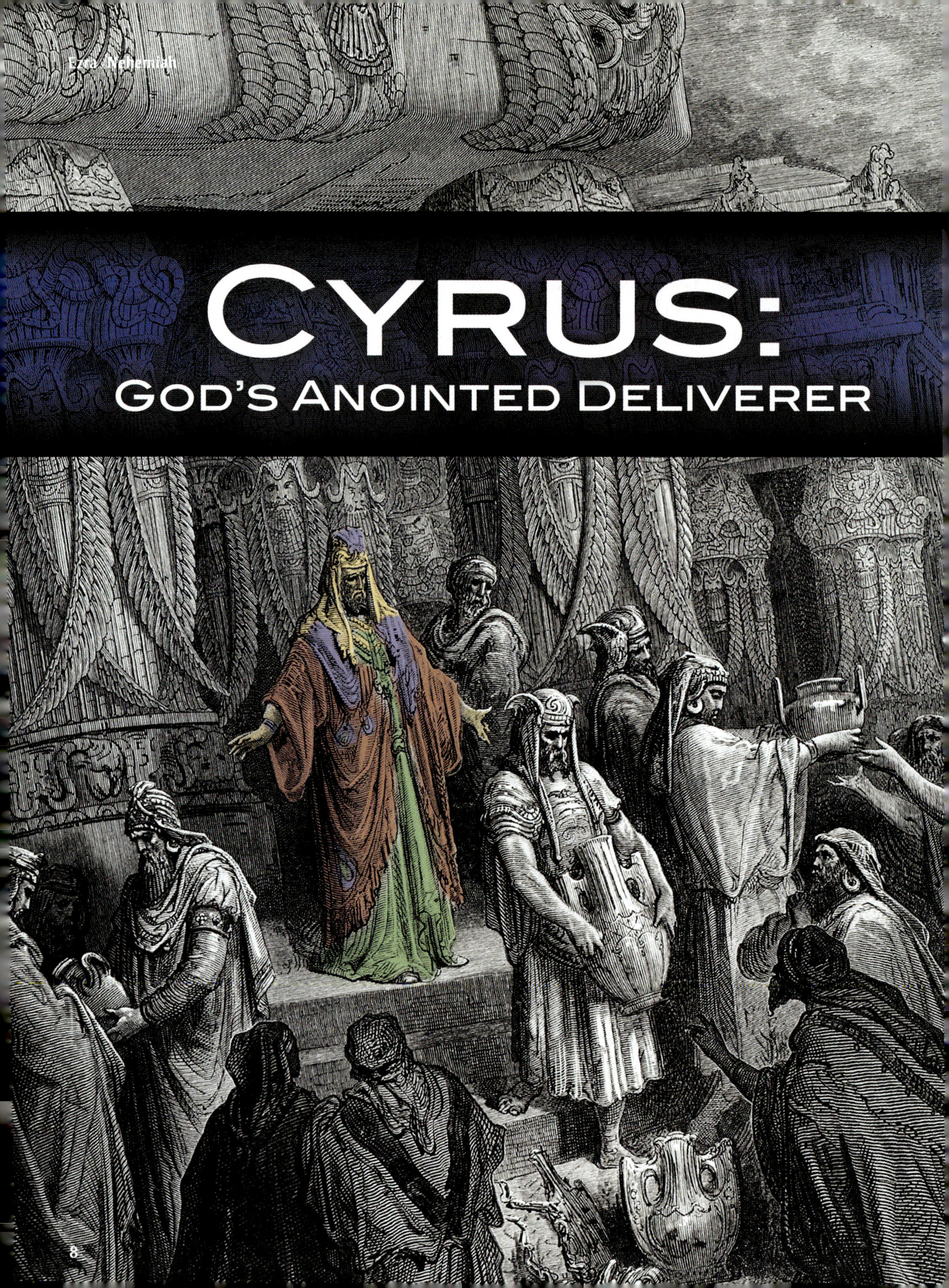

The rebirth of Judah, promised by Jeremiah and Ezekiel, meant that the end of the nation in 587 BC was not actually *the* end. Moses' warnings and those of other eighth-century prophets (e.g., Micah 3:9–12; Isaiah 5:1–7) had come true. But Gospel oracles were also fulfilled. God gave assurances that He would stand by David's household, and He backed up this pledge with His Word. Exile could not be the last word, for God had promised resurrection and life eternal!

Jeremiah declared how this happened. "The Lord has stirred up the spirit of the kings of the Medes [the people to which Cyrus's mother belonged], because His purpose concerning Babylon is to destroy it, for that is the vengeance of the Lord, the vengeance for His temple" (Jeremiah 51:11). In 538 BC, this stirring prompted Cyrus's decree (Ezra 1:2). Not only did Babylon fall to Cyrus, but he also made it possible for the temple to be rebuilt. Historians characterize this Persian leader as one of history's greatest liberators and humanitarians. Cyrus practiced religious toleration on a broad scale.

What more do we know about Cyrus? I'm so glad you asked!

A Mighty Pagan King

In 558 BC, Cyrus began to gain political momentum when, as a minor prince from the province of Anshan, he became head of the Persian tribe in Pasargadae, which was east-southeast of Babylon in the Iranian mountains. Assuming leadership over united Persia by 555 BC, Cyrus successfully rebelled against Media and their capital, Ecbatana, in 550 BC (Isaiah refers to these victories in Isaiah 41:2–7). Also that year, the Median nobility allied with Cyrus and made him the king of Medo-Persia. Shortly after that, he launched another string of spectacular blitzkrieg-like military victories. In 546 BC, Cyrus subjugated Croesus of Lydia and added this country to his rapidly growing kingdom.

This meteoric rise to power was due, in large part, to the failed policies of the last Babylonian monarch, Nabonidus (556–539 BC). He sought to give Babylon a new identity by launching the reconstruction of the Ehulhul temple at Haran and dedicating it to the moon god, Sîn. Nabonidus's decision to spearhead this building program in faraway Syria was a fatal mistake, for it gave more power to the peripheral regions of the empire. This decentralization, in turn, brought on an uprising in the capital city of Babylon. Its citizens resented the fact that Haran had been the last capital of the Assyrian archenemy and that they had promoted the worship of Sîn.

While rebuilding Sîn's temple, Nabonidus lived ten years in Tema, a city in northwestern Arabia. His son Belshazzar became co-regent and ruled from the Babylonian heartland. While Nabonidus avoided Babylon, the Akitu festival became immobilized. Without the king present, this New Year's procession could not proceed. After ten years, and with Cyrus gaining military momentum, Nabonidus returned to Babylon. At the same time, he also implemented another ill-fated policy. The king sought to replace the chief Babylonian god, Marduk, with Sîn.

The response was instant and effective. Marduk's priesthood led the people of Babylon to revolt, labeling Nabonidus a lunatic. Marduk's supporters collaborated with the Persians who were led by one of Cyrus's generals, Gobryas, who entered the city on October 29, 539 BC. He encountered minimal resistance. Cyrus capitalized on the popular mood and staked everything on the Babylonian love for their god Marduk. His first order of business was to show public support for the city's chief deity. Cyrus sent his son Cambyses to take part in the celebration of the Akitu festival after the conquest, thus making it clear that he and his people were true successors of the Babylonian rulers.

An Unlikely Instrument of God

Ezra 1:1–4 narrates the events in early 538 BC, often called "Cyrus's decree." The Cyrus Cylinder, though it does not mention Israel, documents the Persian policy of currying favor with Babylonian captives by sponsoring the rebuilding of temples throughout the empire. The cylinder indicates that, although he acknowledged that "the Lord, the God of heaven, has given me all the kingdoms of the earth, and He has charged me to build Him a house at Jerusalem" (Ezra 1:2), he also believed it was the pagan god Marduk's initiative that made it possible for him to conquer Babylon. At any rate, the Persian allowed Israelites to return to Jerusalem and rebuild the temple. "In the first year of Cyrus the king, Cyrus the king issued a decree: Concerning the house of God at Jerusalem, let the house be rebuilt" (Ezra 6:3). Like David, Cyrus does not complete the task of temple construction. Instead, it is later finished by faithful servants in the generation after the exile: men such as Sheshbazzar, Zerubbabel, Haggai, Zechariah, Ezra, and Nehemiah.

We can only surmise that Isaiah's announcement that Cyrus would be God's "shepherd" (Isaiah 44:28) and "anointed" (Isaiah 45:1) was met with suspicion and cynicism. Discussions could have gone something like this: "If the Lord's 'new thing' (Isaiah 43:19) is a new exodus, then where is a new Moses?" It may have continued, "Why, Moses heard the voice from the burning bush say, 'I am who I am.' This Cyrus doesn't even know the Lord! How can he be our means of salvation?" Others might have chimed in, "Scripture says that God is not done with the line of David. So where is His promise of the everlasting covenant with David?" Finally, the most negative in the group could have protested, "We want a restoration of David! Who is this new upstart king named Cyrus?" The exiles wanted to be saved *their* way, not God's way (see Isaiah 55:8–9).

The Scandal of the Gospel

The Lord's use of Cyrus as His anointed instrument of deliverance was viewed by many as being rather scandalous. After all, God's people having to receive such charity—and from a pagan, no less! It was distasteful, to say the least. It was shameful. Of course, even more shocking is God's use of Jesus, the Anointed One. He was "a stumbling block to Jews and folly to Gentiles" (1 Corinthians 1:23). Paul describes how divine activity takes place. "But God chose what is foolish in the world to shame the wise; God chose what is weak in the world to shame the strong" (1 Corinthians 1:27).

God, in His infinite wisdom, did not give us what we wanted. Rather, He gave us what we truly needed. In our own eyes, our sins are not that drastic, not too severe, not really damning. Therefore, our salvation shouldn't be too hard—it shouldn't be difficult or shameful. Yet God indeed knows the true depth and severity of our sinfulness, and that our sin must be accounted for. So He sent His Son into the world, that on the cross Jesus would bear for us the full and indescribable shame and contempt and horror that we by our sins have deserved. Trusting in Him, we would be delivered; our shame would be wiped away. We see a definite foreshadowing of this in King Cyrus. Through a shameful occurrence, the people's shame was erased, and they went to the Promised Land.

GET OUT of Babylon!

You know, it is said that if a frog is placed in hot water, it will jump out;

Susanna Petroysan heard her daughter cry out, "Mommy, I'm thirsty. I want a drink." She and four-year-old Gayaney were stuck in a basement beneath tons of collapsed concrete and steel. It was December 7, 1988, and an earthquake in Armenia had just killed 45,000 people.

"Mommy, I'm so thirsty. I want a drink."

After feeling around in the darkness of their basement, Susanna found some shattered glass. She used it to slash her finger and then gave it to Gayaney to suck her blood. Days passed. Susanna had no idea how many times she cut her fingers. She only knew that if she stopped, her daughter would die.

Our bondage to a life of conformity begins with just one more drink, one more lie, one more fling, one more glance. But one more always longs for one more, and then just one more.

Hands were cut, blood was shed, and the child was saved.

A monstrous reality called Babylon was a fire-breathing horror that destroyed everything Judah held near and dear. The empire's policy decided once and for all to destroy the "rebellious city, hurtful to kings and provinces" and this is "why this city was laid waste" (Ezra 4:15).

In August 587 BC, Israel's world caved in. The temple collapsed, the monarchy lay in ruins, the land became a wasteland, and all hope was dismantled and destroyed. Then a massive aftershock brought further wreckage and ruin. Seven hundred miles from home, Judah's exiles became trapped in a basement called Babylon.

Stuck in the Basement

In his oracle against the empire, Jeremiah says in part, "It is a land of images, and they are mad over idols" (Jeremiah 50:38). The very name *Babylon* means "gate of the gods." Here was a place that promised heaven on earth! As people entered the massive complex of buildings through the Ishtar Gate and walked onto the great Processional Way, they would step on imported limestone slabs. Each one was inscribed with the phrase "To the honor of Marduk."

Many of Babylon's prisoners of war accepted the empire's indoctrination, namely that the Lord was a non-player and that history was now governed by Babylonian gods. With every passing year, Marduk seemed more powerful and the Lord more incidental. And as Babylon became a hospitable home, some concluded that it was the nerve center of the universe!

The empire trafficked in assimilation and intimidation. For example, in Daniel 1:7, a Babylonian chief official changed the Hebrew names of Daniel, Hananiah, Mishael, and Azariah to Belteshazzar, Shadrach, Meshach, and Abednego. What was the goal? Mark the Judeans with new names that will entice them into worshiping Marduk. Other Hebrews with Babylonian names include Zerubbabel ("offspring of Babylon") the son of Shealtiel, governor who led the exiles back to Judah, and Mordecai (see the Book of Esther), whose name is a Hebrew form of Marduk.

In Daniel 3, the Babylonian king Nebuchadnezzar becomes enraged that Shadrach, Meshach, and Abednego do not acculturate and pledge allegiance to the state. They are thrown into the burning furnace and miraculously come out alive. Yet even with God's protecting care, Ezekiel 20:39 indicates that apostasy was rampant during the Babylonian exile. Many Judean exiles were slow to line up to be marked as belonging to the Lord (see Isaiah 44:5). Babylon seemed to offer so much more! Economic documents from Israelite businesses at Tel el Murassu on the Tigris River show that blending in with Babylon brought with it financial gain. Conformity was the order of the day.

It was the whole boiling-frog syndrome. You know, it is said that if a frog is placed in hot water, it will jump out; but if it is placed in lukewarm water that is gradually heated, it will never get out but will slowly die.

Though in 538 BC, Ezra tells us that 42,360 faithful Israelites left Babylon, along with 7,337 menservants and maidservants, 200 men and women singers, 736 horses, 245 mules, 435 camels, and 6,720 donkeys (Ezra 2:64–67).

Can you just imagine how those who didn't travel to Jerusalem responded to the call to go home? "Haven't you heard? Babylon is the political-military-religious superpower of the day! This is the land of life, liberty, and the purchase of happiness! Why should we go back to little backwater Judah? Besides, what a huge hassle it would be to liquidate our assets, pack our bags, and pull up stakes just to live in a land devastated by famine and warfare. Get out of Babylon? You must be kidding! Get lost!"

Our bondage to a life of conformity begins with just one more drink, one more lie, one more fling, one more glance. But one more always longs for one more, and then just one more. And then a massive earthquake hits, and in its aftershocks we find ourselves trapped in a basement called Babylon.

What next?

The boiling-frog syndrome unleashes its hypnotic power!

Sure, being obsessed with money, gossip, food, Internet ›ornography, people's approval, or work is a strange place to be n, at first. It's crushing to be trapped beneath tons of collapsed ›opes and shattered dreams.

But in time, we become accustomed to living in destruction nd death. With each passing day, it becomes easier to deny hat we are stuck on stuff that kills and steals and destroys. We re in hot water!

It's in God's heart to call people out of darkness and into His marvelous light. He called Abram and Sarai to get out of Haran because it was the center of moon worship. He urged Lot and his family to get out of Sodom and Gomorrah because t was the center of sexual perversion. He called Israel to get ›ut of Egypt because it was the epicenter of a socialization that ›rought about massive dehumanization. You see, at the core of srael's narrative is the Lord's ongoing call for His people to get ›ut of decadence, decay, and death.

Preserved by Blood

Deep down, we're all thirsty, but not for more of the same. We know the water in the desert is saltwater. It doesn't quench; it kills. No. We are thirsty for a clean conscience, a fresh start, for a loving, tender hand to reach into our basement and get us out.

Jesus alone is able to reach into our wreckage, and He does it with hands laced with blood. Finally, you see, blood was all Jesus had. His disciples had deserted Him. His garments had been gambled away. Even His Father had turned His back. Blood was all He had, but the blood of Jesus is all we need.

Hands were cut, blood was shed, and we are saved.

And our response?

We get out of Babylon, we flee Chaldea, and we declare it with a shout of joy.

He called Israel to get out of Egypt because it was the epicenter of a socialization that brought about massive dehumanization. You see, at the core of Israel's narrative is the Lord's ongoing call for His people to get out of decadence, decay, and death.

kphoto.com

THE SACRED VESSELS

"Daddy?"

A little hand touched my forehead. I opened my eyes, which happened to be fixed on the digital clock by our bed. It read 1:45—that would be a.m.

"Yes, Jonathan."

"I need to go to the bathroom."

"Fine, pal. Thanks for the update!"

Jonathan was four at the time. Our home had just been remodeled, and the bathroom was now down a long hallway. When you are four years old and wandering around the house at night, a new hallway looks five miles long with multiple side rooms, where giants are waiting to jump out and eat little kids for late-night snacks.

"Daddy?"

"Yes, Jonathan."

"Please come with me?"

"Thanks for the invitation, son, but for some reason I'm tired. You go ahead."

Shuffle. Shuffle. Stop. Turn around. Shuffle back.

"Daddy?"

"Yes, son."

"Please go with me?"

"Okay."

So I crawled out of bed and we walked together. You see, Jonathan was longing for human presence. He didn't want to be alone.

And neither did the post-exilic community in the Persian province of Yehud (the Persian term for Judah). One way God's presence and blessing came to them was through the liturgical vessels from Solomon's temple. This is why Isaiah writes these words to those who would leave Babylon and return to Jerusalem. "Depart, depart, go out from there; touch no unclean thing; go out from the midst of her; purify yourselves, you who bear the vessels of the Lord" (Isaiah 52:11). Once the temple was rebuilt, the sacred vessels would be needed to resume the sacrificial system, deliver God's forgiveness, and assure His people of His gracious presence. They would not be alone!

God's Presence among His People

In 705 BC, the Judean king Hezekiah displayed the temple vessels to a Babylonian visiting party, led by Merodach-baladan, son of Baladan, king of Babylon, and Isaiah responded with the promise that they would be carried off to Babylon (Isaiah 39). In fulfillment of the prophet's words, in 587 BC, Nebuchadnezzar carried off the gold vessels and other articles that Solomon had made for the temple; he then placed the vessels in his palace in Babylon (2 Chronicles 36:7).

It was common in the ancient Near East for victors to seize images of the gods of the people they had defeated. Since the First Commandment forbade the making of the Lord's image, there was nothing the Babylonians could take. Therefore, they confiscated Judah's liturgical vessels.

Jeremiah has much more to say about this. He writes that the vessels were seized when King Jehoiachin was deported in 597 BC. He also confronts the false prophets of his day who said that the confiscated containers would quickly return to Jerusalem. Instead, the prophet maintained that the vessels would remain in Babylon for seventy years. After that time, the Lord would bring His vessels back. The return of the sacred containers, then, would be a sign that the Lord was with His people. He was going to reside again in the new temple, and the sacrificial life of Israel would begin again. (See Jeremiah 25 and 27 for details.)

The Lord made good on His Word when benevolent Persian king Cyrus entrusted his treasurer, Mithredath, to give the vessels to "Sheshbazzar the prince of Judah" (Ezra 1:8). This was such a monumental event that it was accompanied by official governmental actions, including an official memorandum and an inventory. Ezra subsequently turns the containers over to twelve priests: Sherebiah, Hashabiah, and ten of their relatives (Ezra 8:24).

The list of the vessels is impressive. "And this was the number of them: 30 basins of gold, 1,000 basins of silver, 29 censers, 30 bowls of gold, 410 bowls of silver, and 1,000 other vessels; all the vessels of gold and of silver were 5,400" (Ezra 1:9–11).

Those who returned from Babylon were deeply conscious of the ancestry of their faith, and this made them aware of the problem of continuity with that faith. Therefore, they made use of the vessels to make good their claim to be the true successors of God's promises to Israel (perhaps in this way to invalidate the contrary claims of others; see Nehemiah 2:19). The vessels of Solomon meant that those who now returned were the same people of God as those who worshiped there in earlier times. They were the true descendants of Abraham, Isaac, and Jacob. The holy containers signaled God's presence among His people.

With Us Always

So often in our lives, we can feel as though we have been forgotten or left alone. So often, it can seem that God is distant from us; perhaps He has even washed His hands of us and left us. However, no matter how things may ever seem or appear, we can know that is never the case.

God indeed is with us always. God's presence even "became flesh and dwelt among us, and we have seen His glory" (John 1:14). Coming down past the galaxies, past the solar systems, past the moon and the stars, Jesus became flesh and appeared in the silence of a night, in the warmth of a stable, and in the whisper of a baby. Here is majesty in the midst of the mundane; holiness in the filth of cattle manure; the Deity entering the world on the floor of a barn, through the womb of a teenager and in the presence of a carpenter. Jesus took on flesh so that He might take us into His arms, heal our hurts, forgive our filth, and destroy our darkness. He took on flesh, not to demonstrate the innocence of infancy, but in order to live the life we could not and die our death so we need not. He is Immanuel—God with us.

Like Ezra and Nehemiah before us, we have been given visual reminders of this. The next time you approach the altar to receive Christ's true body and blood, look at the vessels. The flagon and chalice deliver His blood, while the paten holds His precious body. The sacred containers hold God's real presence for you in Jesus Christ. God makes this promise to you: "I will never leave you nor forsake you" (Hebrews 13:5). In fact, nothing "in all creation, will be able to separate us from the love of God in Christ Jesus our Lord" (Romans 8:39). Then, as you walk down your next long, dark hallway, rest assured. You are not alone!

So often it can seem that God is distant from us; perhaps He has even washed His hands of us and left us. However, no matter how things may ever seem or appear, we can know that is never the case.

Study Guide

Cover illustration: © Concordia Publishing House/Greg Copeland

Returning from Exile

Deuteronomy 29–30; 2 Chronicles 36; Ezekiel 36; Jeremiah 25:1–14; Daniel 1; 5; Esther 2; 4; Isaiah 45

Distribute before session 1 for use in session 1.

Use enrichment magazine pp. 2–7.

Resources for Worship

Use these resources for your daily study at home and at the week's assembly.

Hymn

To God the Holy Spirit let us pray
For the true faith needed on our way
That He may defend us when life is ending
And from exile home we are wending.
Lord, have mercy!

O sweetest Love, Your grace on us bestow;
Set our hearts with sacred fire aglow
That with hearts united we love each other,
Ev'ry stranger, sister, and brother.
Lord, have mercy!

Transcendent Comfort in our ev'ry need,
Help us neither scorn nor death to heed
That we may not falter nor courage fail us
When the foe shall taunt and assail us.
Lord, have mercy!
(*LSB* 768:1–3)

Prayer

Merciful, heavenly Father, when You brought the remnant of Your chosen people back from their exile, it was more than just giving them a second chance. You were keeping Your promise of salvation through Jesus Christ and preparing the hearts of those who would receive Him in faith. Grant us now, as we see Your gracious hand in the events of our lives, that we may be strengthened in our faithfulness, and draw us ever closer to the heavenly city that You have prepared for all Your ransomed people, through Jesus Christ, our Lord. Amen.

Digging Deep
My Personal Study for Week 1

Before we start digging into the Books of Ezra and Nehemiah, we will use this week to learn some of the Israelite history that led to the events in our study. Over this first week, we will take a look at what led to the exile in the first place and at some of the main characters from that time.

Day 1 • Read Deuteronomy 29–30; 2 Chronicles 36:1–16; Ezekiel 36:16–38

1. Read Deuteronomy 29:18–29. Who was the first prophet to pass along God's threat of exile?

2. What was the cause of the Lord's wrath that resulted in the people's exile to Babylon?

3. Read Deuteronomy 30:1–10. What is promised at the end of their time of exile?

4. Read 2 Chronicles 36:1–16 for a recap of the historical events that took place leading up to the Babylonian exile. What was the final decline of Judah?

5. According to Ezekiel 36:16–38, what is God's key motivation in bringing His people back to the Holy Land?

Day 2 • Read 2 Chronicles 36:17–21; Jeremiah 25:1–14; Ezekiel 36:1–15

6. Read Exodus 23:10–12. The Sabbath was intended for people to rest, just as God had done following His creation of the world in six days. They were not to do any work, and the land was not to be tilled or harvested. What were some practical and spiritual purposes for these observances?

7. Read 2 Chronicles 36:17–21. What was going to be accomplished once the people were removed from the land? When would they return?

8. According to Jeremiah 25:1–14, what is the symbolic length of the time of exile? If the king of Babylon is the Lord's "servant" (25:9) then why will he also be punished?

9. Read Ezekiel 36:1–15. What is the unusual addressee receiving the divine Word of promise? Why would God not have Ezekiel direct this prophecy to the people instead?

10. When it is impressed upon God's people that the land still belongs to Him and not to them, then they would be reminded to regard all that they have in their promised inheritance as purely a gift and not as something they own. How does acknowledging God's ownership of everything we call ours help us gain perspective on our role as caretakers of His property?

Return and Rebuild

Ezra 1–3; Leviticus 23:33–43

Distribute before session 2 for use in session 2.

Use enrichment magazine pp. 8–10.

Resources for Worship

Use these resources for your daily study at home and at the week's assembly.

Hymn

May we Thy precepts, Lord, fulfill
And do on earth our Father's will
As angels do above;
Still walk in Christ, the living way,
With all Thy children and obey
The law of Christian love.

So may we join Thy name to bless,
Thy grace adore, Thy pow'r confess,
From sin and strife to flee.
One is our calling, one our name,
The end of all our hopes the same,
A crown of life with Thee.

Spirit of life, of love and peace,
Unite our hearts, our joy increase,
Thy gracious help supply.
To each of us the blessing give
In Christian fellowship to live,
In joyful hope to die.
(*LSB* 698)

Prayer

O Lord, our God, as the foundation was being laid for Jerusalem's second temple, the people's cheering was mingled with tears of sorrow over the loss of the magnificent first temple. When we come to those moments in our lives in which a wonderful blessing is mixed with pain, provide us with Your peace and strength, as only You can give, so that by the Holy Spirit we can gain the proper perspective as we travel our life's journey, and also look forward with joyful anticipation toward the full revelation of the precious salvation that, although hidden now, is already ours in Christ Jesus, our Lord. Amen.

Digging Deep
My Personal Study for Week 2

Day 1 • Read Ezra 1:1–4

1. What two things did Cyrus claim that the Lord did for him?

2. What caused King Cyrus to make these claims?

3. Read Daniel 6:8, 12, 15. When a law or pronouncement was made in Persia, what could be done to overturn it?

4. Why do you think Cyrus's decree focuses only on rebuilding the temple in Jerusalem and does not mention rebuilding the city itself?

5. If a world leader made a similar pronouncement today in support of the Christian faith, how do you think the news media would evaluate it?

Day 2 • Read Ezra 1:5–11

6. What actions of King Cyrus made it clear that he was going to follow through on his decree?

7. The tribes of Judah and Benjamin comprised the former Southern Kingdom. They were nearly the only Israelites left in the Holy Land when Nebuchadnezzar imposed the Babylonian exile. The other ten tribes of the Northern Kingdom had been already decimated and exiled by earlier raids, especially by the Assyrians. Why was this important to the lineage of the coming Messiah? (See Micah 5:2.)

8. Read Numbers 1:48–54 and 1 Chronicles 13. Why was it necessary to include the priests and Levites for this initial return trip to Jerusalem?

9. What were the vessels of silver and gold used for in temple life? How does Ezra 1:6 compare with Exodus 12:35–36?

10. Read Jeremiah 27:19–22. The vessels were returned to Jerusalem along with the exiles. What significance would this have for the Israelites?

Day 3 • Read Ezra 2

11. Into what categories are the returning exiles listed in Ezra 2?

Worship Restored

Ezra 4–6

Distribute before session 3 for use in session 3.

Use enrichment magazine pp. 11–13.

Resources for Worship

Use these resources for your daily study at home and at the week's assembly.

Hymn

With the Lord begin your task;
  Jesus will direct it.
For His aid and counsel ask;
  Jesus will perfect it.
Ev'ry morn with Jesus rise,
  And when day is ended,
In His name then close your eyes;
  Be to Him commended.

Let each day begin with prayer,
  Praise, and adoration.
On the Lord cast ev'ry care;
  He is your salvation.
Morning, evening, and at night
  Jesus will be near you,
Save you from the tempter's might,
  With His presence cheer you.

With your Savior at your side,
  Foes need not alarm you;
In His promises confide,
  And no ill can harm you.
All your trust and hope repose
  In the mighty Master,
Who in wisdom truly knows
  How to stem disaster.

If your task be thus begun
  With the Savior's blessing,
Safely then your course will run,
  Toward the promise pressing.
Good will follow ev'rywhere
  While you here must wander;
You at last the joy will share
  In the mansions yonder.

Thus, Lord Jesus, ev'ry task
  Be to You commended;
May Your will be done, I ask,
  Until life is ended.
Jesus, in Your name begun
  Be the day's endeavor;
Grant that it may well be done
  To Your praise forever.
(*LSB* 869)

Prayer

O God of peace and harmony, our experience in this sin-filled world will remain full of misfortune, violence, and strife until the end of time. Without the forgiveness and mercy that You have shown to us and to the whole earth, we would have been lost eternally and removed from Your blessing. Look upon us with love, and where there is any bitterness or anger, root it out and cleanse our hearts. By Your grace, may we not lose our inheritance in Your kingdom, but rather be ever eager that our enemies be turned in repentance toward You and that in full reconciliation we would share eternal happiness together; through Jesus Christ, our Lord. Amen.

Digging Deep
My Personal Study for Week 3

Day 1 • Read Ezra 4:1–6

1. What did the "adversaries of Judah and Benjamin" request of the Judean leaders in Ezra 4:2? On what basis did they make their request?

2. Why were these enemies, who were Samaritans, prohibited from helping the Jews rebuild the temple?

3. Based on Ezra 4:4–16, what was the enemies' real motive? What could the consequences have been if the Samaritans had started work on the temple project along with the Jews?

4. Read 2 Kings 17:21–41. How did the Samaritan race or sect come about?

5. Read John 4:1–30 and Galatians 3:28. In what ways did the coming of Jesus Christ finally achieve reconciliation with the Samaritans?

Day 2 • Read Ezra 4:7–24

6. What is the desired outcome of the letter written by the officials Rehum and Shimshai, along with all the other signatories, including the Samaritans?

7. What threat does a rebuilt Jerusalem pose to the Persian Empire, as argued by this letter?

8. Who do you think might be examples of the "mighty kings" mentioned in verse 20?

9. Read Jeremiah 24; Micah 1; and Zephaniah 3. In what ways was Jerusalem rightfully to be considered a "rebellious and wicked city" (Ezra 4:12)?

Teach and Pray

Ezra 7–8

Distribute before session 4 for use in session 4.

Use enrichment magazine pp. 14–16.

Resources for Worship

Use these resources for your daily study at home and at the week's assembly.

Hymn

Jerusalem, my happy home,
When shall I come to thee?
When shall my sorrows have an end?
Thy joys when shall I see?

O happy harbor of the saints,
O sweet and pleasant soil!
In thee no sorrow may be found,
No grief, no care, no toil.

Thy gardens and thy gallant walks
Continually are green;
There grow such sweet and pleasant flow'rs
As nowhere else are seen.

There trees forevermore bear fruit
And evermore do spring;
There evermore the angels dwell
And evermore do sing.

Apostles, martyrs, prophets, there
Around my Savior stand;
And soon my friends in Christ below
Will join the glorious band.

O Christ, do Thou my soul prepare
For that bright home of love
That I may see Thee and adore
With all Thy saints above.
(*LSB* 673)

Prayer

Heavenly Father, though our sins are like scarlet, it is by the blood of Your own dear Son, Jesus, that they shall be made whiter than snow. Out of sheer grace, and without any merit or worthiness in ourselves, You give us everything we need both in this body and life, and for the strengthening of our faith for the life to come. Hear our humble cry for forgiveness. Heed the gracious intercession of Christ on our own behalf. Listen to the inexpressible groans that the Holy Spirit offers before Your throne. For we often know not the things for which to pray, yet we thankfully are certain that all we need is ours for the sake of Christ, in whose name we pray, Amen.

Digging Deep
My Personal Study for Week 4

Day 1 • Read Ezra 7:1–10

1. What was Ezra's occupation in addition to being born a priest? What would be involved in his regular work? How would you describe his relationship with the Persian ruler?

2. Compare Ezra's genealogy with the record of Aaron's sons in 1 Chronicles 6:3–14. What do you notice about how the list is recorded? What could be the reason that some names do not appear in both lists?

3. Genealogies help us understand lineage and history. Which genealogical format is closer to Ezra 7: Matthew 1 or Luke 3?

4. Read 1 Corinthians 12:27–13:13. As a Christian considers all parts of his or her calling, what is the number one concern of the believer who, like Ezra, desires to do what is pleasing to God? What benefit can we take from Christ's love toward us?

5. How could an increase in Bible study and prayer improve the way you approach your own various callings in life? See Ezra 7:6, 9 and 2 Samuel 7:3.

Day 2 • Read Ezra 7:11–28

6. What did the Persian king's decree authorize Ezra to do? What special privileges were extended to people involved in the worship activities of the Jerusalem temple?

7. Why would an unbelieving Persian king be so concerned about the proper worship of the Lord in Jerusalem, hundreds of miles away?

8. Christians know from Romans 13 that they should support the government. What is the motivation for a government, from its own perspective, to grant certain privileges (e.g., tax exemption) to churches? Is it merely because they don't make a profit, or is there another reason?

9. Why was Ezra given authority to collect from the neighboring Persian province known as Beyond the River (vv. 21–26)? What earlier king's document had arranged for their taxes, rather than the taxes of the Judeans, to pay for the renovation of Jerusalem and its temple?

10. Ezra gained great encouragement when he knew that "the hand of the Lord [his] God was on [him]" (7:28). What gives you the strongest confidence that God is pleased to bless the work you do?

Restore Purity

Ezra 9–10

Distribute before session 5 for use in session 5.

Use enrichment magazine pp. 17–19.

Resources for Worship

Use these resources for your daily study at home and at the week's assembly.

Hymn

From depths of woe I cry to Thee,
In trial and tribulation;
Bend down Thy gracious ear to me,
Lord, hear my supplication.
If Thou rememb'rest ev'ry sin,
Who then could heaven ever win
Or stand before Thy presence?

Thy love and grace alone avail
To blot out my transgression;
The best and holiest deeds must fail
To break sin's dread oppression.
Before Thee none can boasting stand,
But all must fear Thy strict demand
And live alone by mercy.

Therefore my hope is in the Lord
And not in mine own merit;
It rests upon His faithful Word
To them of contrite spirit
That He is merciful and just;
This is my comfort and my trust.
His help I wait with patience.
(*LSB* 607:1–3)

Prayer

Create in us a pure heart, O God, and renew a right spirit within us. Cast us not away from Your presence, and take not Your Holy Spirit from us. Restore to us the joy of Your salvation and uphold us with Your free Spirit. Purify our hearts so that we would know nothing but the truth of Your Word, and preserve us from sin and temptation. Keep us from accommodating to our selfish, sin-centered world, and awaken in us a genuine love for those who are caught in the entanglements of anxiety and weak faith. As You have forgiven us in Christ, so move us by the Spirit to be ready to forgive those who have trespassed against us. May it be so for Jesus' sake. Amen.

Digging Deep
My Personal Study for Week 5

Day 1 • Read Ezra 9:1–9

1. What was the danger that Ezra saw when it was reported to him that some Israelites had intermarried with people of other nationalities?

2. Read Ruth 1:15–18 and 4:11–12. Why is Ruth, who is also an outsider to the Israelite people, allowed to marry Boaz? What is the difference in her case?

3. The term "holy race" in verse 2 could also be translated "holy seed" or "holy offspring," referring to the promise of Christ (see Galatians 3:16). How would mixing with different religions adversely affect the lineage that would eventually lead to Jesus?

4. As Ezra begins his prayer of confession, how does he describe God's grace? Why do our worship services begin with a corporate confession and forgiveness of sins, followed by the Kyrie ("Lord, have mercy")?

5. What challenges do you think a couple could face in a marriage where the two are of different faiths or different confessions of Christianity? How is this different from a couple where the two believe the same way?

Day 2 • Read Ezra 9:10–15

6. In Ezra's prayer, what was the connection between the religions of other nations and the purity of the land?

7. Read Ezekiel 18:1–4, 19–23. What was the meaning of the proverb "The fathers have eaten sour grapes, and the children's teeth are set on edge"? How is Ezekiel's commentary on personal responsibility for sin applied in Ezra's prayer of confession?

8. Read Deuteronomy 7:1–20 and 9:4–5. What was the original reason for the Israelites to destroy the other people who were living in the Promised Land?

9. When the Old Testament prophets refer to the people of Israel as a "remnant," they do so to either emphasize God's judgment in paring them down to a small number (Law; as in Isaiah 10:19) or His mercy and future promise of the Savior (Gospel; as in Jeremiah 23:3). Which do you think is the greater emphasis on the term "remnant" in Ezra's prayer (v. 14)?

10. Ezra offered his prayer in the evening, at the time of sacrifice. What is fitting about confessing sins to God and one another at the end of the day? See Psalm 4:4–8; Ephesians 4:25–32; and Matthew 5:23–24.

Courage to Speak

Nehemiah 1–2

Distribute before session 6 for use in session 6

Use enrichment magazine pp. 20–22.

Resources for Worship

Use these resources for your daily study at home and at the week's assembly.

Hymn

Fight the good fight with all your might;
Christ is your strength, and Christ your right.
Lay hold on life, and it shall be
Your joy and crown eternally.

Run the straight race through God's good grace;
Lift up your eyes, and seek His face.
Life with its way before us lies;
Christ is the path, and Christ the prize.

Cast care aside, lean on your guide;
His boundless mercy will provide.
Trust, and enduring faith shall prove
Christ is your life and Christ your love.

Faint not nor fear, His arms are near;
He changes not who holds you dear;
Only believe, and you will see
That Christ is all eternally.
(*LSB* 664)

Prayer

Almighty God, our Creator and Redeemer, You have given us body and soul and all that we have. The talents, abilities, and resources that we count on are gifts from Your most gracious hand. Forgive us when we selfishly claim our own achievement for blessings that You have given us, and also forgive us for the times we have complained to You after encountering failures. Increase our confidence in You, rather than ourselves—a confidence that is daily strengthened as we remember our Baptism into Christ's death and resurrection. Renew our strength to serve in Your name, for the good of Your eternal kingdom, through Jesus Christ, our Lord. Amen.

Digging Deep
My Personal Study for Week 6

Day 1 • Read Nehemiah 1:1–3

1. What was Nehemiah's concern for the city of Jerusalem? What could be a reason that Nehemiah did not already return there with the other Judean exiles?

2. Read Isaiah 40:1–8, 29–31. The Hebrew word for "comfort" is part of Nehemiah's name. What is comforting about Isaiah's prophecy? Why is there comfort specifically for Jerusalem?

3. Compare Nehemiah 1:1–3 with Ezra 4:23–24. Why would it be necessary to resume building Jerusalem's city wall as soon as possible?

4. Read Isaiah 4:2–4; 11:1–10; and 37:30–32. How would you summarize the promises intended for a remnant of God's people who would return to the land of Israel?

5. Read Acts 15:13–18. What does the coming of Jesus Christ mean for the remnant of believers, including Gentiles? including you?

Day 2 • Read Nehemiah 1:4–11

6. What is Nehemiah asking for in his prayer? Why does he include a confession of sin along with his requests?

7. What attribute or quality of God gives Nehemiah the courage to ask Him for an answer to his prayer?

8. Reread Ezra 9:6–15. What are some similar elements between this prayer and that of Nehemiah 1:5–11?

9. Read Hebrews 11:24–26. What comparison could you make between Moses' rejection of prestige and wealth in Egypt and Nehemiah's prayer on behalf of his people while serving in the Persian court?

10. Study a written prayer or psalm from your Bible. Point out as many different parts of it as you can: What name of God is used? For what explicit reason or rationale is the prayer offered? What is the specific request? How does the prayer end?

Rebuild the Wall

Nehemiah 3–7

Distribute before session 7 for use in session 7.

Use enrichment magazine pp. 23–25.

Resources for Worship

Use these resources for your daily study at home and at the week's assembly.

Hymn

Rise! To arms! With prayer employ you,
O Christians, lest the foe destroy you;
For Satan has designed your fall.
Wield God's Word, the weapon glorious;
Against all foes be thus victorious,
For God protects you from them all.
Fear not the hordes of hell,
Here is Emmanuel.
Hail the Savior!
The strong foes yield
To Christ, our shield,
And we, the victors, hold the field.

Cast afar this world's vain pleasure
And boldly strive for heav'nly treasure.
Be steadfast in the Savior's might.
Trust the Lord, who stands beside you,
For Jesus from all harm will hide you.
By faith you conquer in the fight.
Take courage, weary soul!
Look forward to the goal!
Joy awaits you.
The race well run,
Your long war won,
Your crown shines splendid as the sun.

Wisely fight, for time is fleeting;
The hours of grace are fast retreating;
Short, short is this our earthly way.
When the Lord the dead will waken
And sinners all by fear are shaken,
The saints with joy will greet that day.
Praise God, our triumph's sure.
We need not long endure
Scorn and trial.
Our Savior King
His own will bring
To that great glory which we sing.
(*LSB* 668)

Prayer

Lord of Hosts, Your enemies seem to constantly be trying to ambush us, Your chosen people in Christ, and they threaten to halt the work of the Kingdom with which You have entrusted us. How long, O Lord, will Your precious Word be treated like trash in our world around us? We repent that we have not always spoken up for what is pure, true, and good, and instead only served our own personal needs. Vindicate the integrity of Your triune name, and rescue the people who have been baptized into that name. Lead us to look forward with joyful and unashamed expectation for the coming of our Lord Jesus, who will be the final judge over the living and the dead. In His name we pray. Amen.

Digging Deep
My Personal Study for Week 7

Day 1 • Read Nehemiah 3

1. Which gate of the city is found at the beginning and end of the list of work crews? On which parts of the wall were the priests involved? Where does the record list some women as builders?

2. Read 2 Samuel 5:1–12. Who lived in Jerusalem before the Israelites? How did the stronghold of Zion come to be known as the City of David?

3. Read Leviticus 4, noting especially verses 11–12. What was the last necessary step after an animal was sacrificed on the altar? What do you suppose was located outside Jerusalem's Dung Gate?

4. Read 2 Kings 16:3; 23:10; and Leviticus 18:21. What was the detestable pagan practice that had taken place in the Hinnom Valley south of Jerusalem? Why was it constantly smoldering and burning?

5. The rubbish fires in the Valley of Hinnom (Greek: *Gehenna*) were never extinguished. Jesus use this well-known burning rubbish pit as an illustration in Matthew 5:22 and 18:9; to what does He equate it?

Day 2 • Read Nehemiah 4

6. What were the adversaries' methods of discouraging the builders in Nehemiah 4? How did Nehemiah and the people respond?

7. Why was it necessary for everyone to be armed, both the guards and the builders? Why did Nehemiah have to order people to stay the night in the city (4:22)?

8. Review the story of David and Goliath in 1 Samuel 17:23–49. How did David interpret Goliath's words that were spoken against the army of Israel? What did Nehemiah desire when he prayed to God, referring to the taunts of his enemies?

9. Compare Nehemiah's response to ridicule with what Jude reports concerning the archangel Michael in a dispute with the devil (Jude 8–13).

Renew the Covenant

Nehemiah 8–10

Distribute before session 8 for use in session 8.

Use enrichment magazine pp. 26–29.

Resources for Worship

Use these resources for your daily study at home and at the week's assembly.

Hymn

The will of God is always best
And shall be done forever;
And they who trust in Him are blest;
He will forsake them never.
He helps indeed
In time of need;
He chastens with forbearing.
They who depend
On God, their friend,
Shall not be left despairing.

God is my comfort and my trust,
My hope and life abiding;
And to His counsel, wise and just,
I yield, in Him confiding.
The very hairs,
His Word declares,
Upon my head He numbers.
By night and day
God is my stay;
He never sleeps nor slumbers.

Lord, this I ask, O hear my plea,
Deny me not this favor:
When Satan sorely troubles me,
Then do not let me waver.
O guard me well,
My fear dispel,
Fulfill Your faithful saying:
All who believe
By grace receive
An answer to their praying.

When life's brief course on earth is run
And I this world am leaving,
Grant me to say, "Your will be done,"
Your faithful Word believing.
My dearest Friend,
I now commend
My soul into Your keeping;
From sin and hell,
And death as well,
By You the vict'ry reaping.
(*LSB* 758)

Prayer

O God, the everlasting king, as we remember Your generous providence extended toward us, our family members, and Your whole Church throughout all ages, we are moved to render humble thanksgiving for all You have done. When You have chastened us through difficult times, You have always restored and blessed us. We pray that when the fiery trial is done, or the effect of the mountaintop experience subsides, You would remind us that You are present with us also during the "plain" times, so that our faith in You will not go cold or complacent. By Your Holy Spirit, grant us the fire of love for Your Word and for service to our neighbor, through our Lord Jesus Christ. Amen.

Digging Deep
My Personal Study for Week 8

Day 1 • Read Nehemiah 8:1–8

1. Read Leviticus 23:23–25; Numbers 29:1–6; and Deuteronomy 31:10–13. What was to be done at the Feast of Trumpets? For what upcoming festivals, also occurring in the seventh month, were the people to prepare?

2. Skim the exposition on the Law of Moses (the Torah): in Acts 7:1–44. What historical accounts does Stephen reference? How does that history support his point?

3. Read Hebrews 4:12 and 2 Timothy 2:15. The biblical phrases "two-edged sword" and "rightly handling the word of truth" point us to the clear distinctions that need to be made between Law and Gospel. If you were in the crowd listening to Ezra's preaching, what comforting message do you suppose you would be looking for in his explanation of the Torah?

4. Read 2 Timothy 3:14–17 and 1 Peter 3:15. How could you use these passages to answer someone who tells you that learning the Bible is only for pastors and church workers?

5. Nehemiah 8:5–6 gives some liturgical actions of the people. Name three customs and practices that your church observes during the worship service, and find out what each of them is meant to teach about God's Word and the Sacraments.

Day 2 • Read Nehemiah 8:9–18

6. Why were Nehemiah, Ezra, and other leaders making the people stop their crying and mourning during the sacred assembly?

7. What did the people not fully understand about this gathering on the first day of this holy seventh month? Recalling Leviticus 16:29–30, what will be done about their sins on the tenth day of the month?

8. Read Ecclesiastes 3:1–8; 1 Thessalonians 4:13–18; and Matthew 6:16–18. When is it appropriate to mourn? What should be avoided?

9. One person attends Holy Communion with head bowed, eyes closed, and a silent prayer for forgiveness, while another looks up, smiling with joy. What makes both responses appropriate? At what point does one or the other turn into "too much"?

Remember Me, O God!

Nehemiah 11–13

Distribute before session 9 for use in session 9.

Use enrichment magazine pp. 30–32.

Resources for Worship

Use these resources for your daily study at home and at the week's assembly.

Hymn

Why should cross and trial grieve me?
  Christ is near
  With His cheer;
Never will He leave me.
Who can rob me of the heaven
  That God's Son
  For me won
When His life was given?

When life's troubles rise to meet me,
  Though their weight
  May be great,
They will not defeat me.
God, my loving Savior, sends them;
  He who knows
  All my woes
Knows how best to end them.

God gives me my days of gladness,
  And I will
  Trust Him still
When He sends me sadness.
God is good; His love attends me
  Day by day,
  Come what may,
Guides me and defends me.
(*LSB* 756:1–3)

Prayer

Heavenly Father, we can identify with the abundant joy and sense of relief when a major project has been completed. Just as we have studied how the rebuilding of Jerusalem's temple and city wall led to a similar spiritual transition in the hearts and minds of the returning Israelite exiles, so lead us to see a similar inner rebuilding take effect inside us through repentance and faith. Send us capable teachers of Your Word to distribute the gifts of Your grace toward us in Christ. Grant us courageous and faithful leaders in the realms of both church and state, so that we may enjoy the blessings that You have set aside for us; through Jesus Christ, our Lord, who lives and reigns with You and the Holy Spirit, one God, now and forever. Amen.

Digging Deep
My Personal Study for Week 9

Day 1 • Read Nehemiah 11

1. Some Israelites were assigned to live in Jerusalem, and the rest were sent to live in other villages. What do you think the purpose was of this split?

2. Read Numbers 26:52–56; 1 Samuel 10:20–21; and Acts 1:24–26. What was the purpose for casting lots? Why were the people chosen by lot in Nehemiah 11 praised for having volunteered to move to Jerusalem?

3. What is a tithe? How are the tithes described in Nehemiah 10 and 11 related?

4. Read Isaiah 48:1–2; 52:1–2; Matthew 4:5; 27:53; and Revelation 21:1–4. For what reason was Jerusalem called the "holy city"? Should it be considered a holy city now? Why or why not?

5. Read Leviticus 25:8–28. What happened to an Israelite's land during the Year of Jubilee? How did this ensure a lasting inheritance for God's exiled people now returning to the Promised Land?

Day 2 • Read Nehemiah 12:1–30

6. How does this final list of priests and Levites eligible to serve at the temple fit in with the narrative of the city wall's dedication?

7. Review the discussion about lineage in Session 4, Day 1. Why were genealogies so important to the status and work of priests and Levites?

8. Read Acts 14:21–23 and Titus 1:5–9. How are pastors chosen in the Church of the New Testament era, in contrast to genealogical descent?

9. The phrase "apostolic succession" refers today to the supposed requirement, similar to a genealogy, that a legitimate priest must be ordained by someone on whom hands were laid, going back in time by an unbroken chain to the apostles themselves. Based on Isaiah 28:16 and Ephesians 2:19–22, what is the true apostolic succession?

10. Read Leviticus 14:48–53 and Numbers 8:5–7. What was the cleansing ritual for Israelite houses and people? What would the ritual cleansing of the city wall signify?

Day 3 • Read Nehemiah 12:31–47

11. How did the Israelite people celebrate the dedication of the city wall? How were Ezra and Nehemiah involved in the ceremony?

12. Why did the celebration conclude at the temple? How does this event compare with the temple's foundation-laying ceremony in Ezra 3:10–13?

13. Read 2 Samuel 6:12–23 and 1 Chronicles 15:25–29. Why did David dance before the ark of the covenant? What made his wife Michal look upon him with contempt?

14. Read 1 Chronicles 6:31–48; 25:1–8; and 2 Chronicles 35:13–19. Who was Asaph? What was his role under the leadership of King David? How far does his family line extend in the historical record?

15. Which of the twelve psalms attributed to Asaph (Psalms 50 and 73–83) would you choose as most appropriate to the occasion of the dedication of Jerusalem's wall? Why? Prepare to discuss your reasons and examples with the group.

Day 4 • Read Nehemiah 13:1–14

16. What aspect of temple purity was discovered to have been overlooked in Nehemiah 13:1–3?

17. Where was Nehemiah when all these abuses were taking place?

18. Who gave the enemy Tobiah living quarters in the temple chamber where the tithes were supposed to be kept? What did Nehemiah do to remedy the situation and ensure that it wasn't repeated?

19. What forced the Levites to leave the service of the temple and farm their own fields to feed their families? Do you think this could apply to the duty of congregations today to pay their pastors a living wage? Why or why not?

20. Why, when it is true that we are saved by grace without works, would we want to follow the example of Nehemiah and pray that God would remember our good deeds (v. 14)?

Day 5 • Read Nehemiah 13:15–31

21. What sort of Sabbath-Day abuses did Nehemiah discover when he returned to the city of Jerusalem? What was the problem with Tyrians, who were foreigners, selling fish on the Sabbath?

22. What motivated Nehemiah to act so drastically against people guilty of ceremonial abuses such as working on the Sabbath and intermarrying with people who did not know the Hebrew language?

23. Read Mark 2:23–3:6. In what ways did the Pharisees twist Nehemiah's legitimate concern for the Sabbath? What does Jesus mean when He says that the Sabbath was made for man and the Son of Man is Lord of the Sabbath?

24. What examples of faith and piety for Godly laypeople can you find in the life and work of Nehemiah?

Day 3 • Read Nehemiah 9:1–25

10. Why were all foreigners excluded from the Israelite congregation prior to their confession of sin?

11. Compare Nehemiah 9:6–25 with the historical review found in Psalm 136. What are some of the key events mentioned?

12. Why do you think this prayer is more comprehensive than other remembrances of God's past works for the sake of His people?

13. Examine how the same confession of the Lord's grace is applied to different contexts for each of the following: Exodus 34:6; Nehemiah 9:17; Joel 2:13; Jonah 4:2. What is emphasized in each instance? How is this common statement different from our creeds?

14. If you were to add an Old Testament story of your choice to the prayer in Nehemiah 9, what would it be? Why?

Day 4 • Read Nehemiah 9:26–38

15. What was the recurring cycle that the prayer in Nehemiah 9 makes plain to all the people? What is pointed out as constant?

16. The people's prayer of confession included their kings at the front of the list of ancestors who rebelled against the Lord. Why did the people in Jerusalem not reestablish the Israelite monarchy with Nehemiah?

17. What were the limitations placed upon Israelite kings in Deuteronomy 17:14–20?

18. Read 1 Samuel 8. If the Lord allowed Israel to have a king, then why did Samuel counsel against it? What sin did the people commit?

19. What makes confession of sin an essential ingredient in Christian prayer, even for prayers where no sins are explicitly mentioned?

Day 5 • Read Nehemiah 10

20. What would be necessary in order to solidify the rebirth of faith and devotion to God's Word among the Jewish people?

21. If people are saved by God's grace and not by works, then why are the people imposing obligations on themselves in Nehemiah 10?

22. What are some examples of Godly and helpful vows that Christians can make to ensure the proper exercise of their faith?

23. Why were Nehemiah and the other government officials, in addition to the priests and Levites, involved in imposing the covenant on the people following the prayer of confession?

24. If you have access to the resources, research the various U.S. presidents' Thanksgiving Day proclamations, especially those of George Washington and Abraham Lincoln. Without blurring the distinction between secular and sacred, what is a leader's proper role in encouraging a healthy spiritual life?

10. What evidence is there that Nehemiah led by example and didn't simply hand down orders to others? What sort of leader would you prefer to follow?

Day 3 • Read Nehemiah 5

11. What was the problem brought before Nehemiah while he was working on the city-wall project? How did he solve it?

12. Read 1 Samuel 15:26–28; Ezekiel 4:1–8; and Jeremiah 19:1–13. Explain how each example used an object lesson (as in Nehemiah 5:13) to proclaim God's prophetic message.

13. Nehemiah challenges the people to care for the poor. Read James 2:1–10 and 5:1–6. What spiritual benefit does James cite for Christians who take care of the poor? What is the tendency of the sinful human nature?

14. Just as the people spoke an "Amen" in verse 13 to Nehemiah, what did the people mean when they spoke an "Amen" at the end of each verse in Deuteronomy 27:15–26?

15. Read Luke 19:1–10. Zacchaeus was entitled by the Roman government, as a chief tax collector, to extort extra money from the people, but he vowed to Jesus to pay everything back fourfold. Read Luther's explanation to the Ninth Commandment. What other "way which only appears right" can you think of that might tempt someone to seek personal gain through the church?

Day 4 • Read Nehemiah 6:1–14

16. What was the plot designed to attack Nehemiah in an unprotected location?

17. What was especially damaging to Nehemiah on Sanballat's fifth attempt, when he used an open letter?

18. Read Deuteronomy 18:20–22; Matthew 7:15–20; and 1 John 4:1–6. How could people, both good and bad, pick up on who was proclaiming an authentic prophecy and who was a false prophet?

19. Read 1 Samuel 9:15–10:1; 16:1–13; 2 Samuel 12:24–25; and 1 Kings 1:28–40. What was the prophet's role when a new king was named?

20. In Nehemiah 6:10–12, what convinced Nehemiah that Shemaiah would betray him? See Numbers 18:7.

Day 5 • Read Nehemiah 6:15–7:73

21. How did the enemy Tobiah secure an opportunity to subvert Nehemiah and the Jerusalem wall-rebuilding project?

22. What led the nations surrounding Judah to perceive that God had helped Nehemiah and the people build the wall?

23. Review Ezra 9. What comparisons could you make between those who were loyal to Tobiah, yet also rebuilding the wall, and those who had rejected believing wives for those who were unbelieving?

24. Nehemiah claimed that God had prompted him to enroll the people. What differences can you find with the census that King David took in 1 Chronicles 21? How was faith in the Lord involved in each story?

25. Discuss which is easier: to delegate important tasks to trustworthy individuals or to do everything yourself. If you could recruit a man like Nehemiah for work at your church, what task would you assign to him? Why?

Day 3 • Read Nehemiah 2:1–8

11. What is Nehemiah's cause for fear as he approaches King Artaxerxes with his request?

12. How would Nehemiah's position as cupbearer afford him an ideal opportunity to ask the king, when the time was right? Compare this with the opportunity that was given to Esther (Esther 4:14; 7:1–8).

13. Have you offered a short, spontaneous prayer in the midst of a difficult or stressful situation? If so, what comfort or help did you receive from the Lord? In what other situations in your daily life do you think a brief, silent prayer would be appropriate?

14. What were the purposes for the letters that Nehemiah requested to accompany him on his journey to Jerusalem? Who was friendly in receiving Nehemiah and his letter? Who was not?

15. Why would Nehemiah have refrained from mentioning Jerusalem by name? What is the significance of the substitute phrase "the city of my fathers' graves"?

Day 4 • Read Nehemiah 2:9–16

16. Do you think Nehemiah asked for a military escort? What was different between his journey and Ezra's that called for this form of protection?

17. Is it a contradiction to trust in God above all things and yet make use of His earthly means to provide security, sustenance, or even justice? What distinctions should be kept clear?

18. How would you compare or contrast the adversaries and their actions listed in Nehemiah 2:10 with those mentioned in Ezra 4:1–2, 7–16; 5:6–17?

19. What connection can you draw between Nehemiah's secret examination of Jerusalem's walls and Jesus' warning not to tell anyone about Him (e.g., see Mark 1:43–45)?

20. On the one hand, we in God's kingdom should not be surprised that there is persecution of the saints (Luke 6:22–23; 2 Timothy 3:12; 1 Peter 3:17). On the other hand, we are advised not to invite it upon ourselves needlessly (Proverbs 4:14–17; Luke 22:35–38). How can we determine when we should suffer and when we should fight in our spiritual battles?

Day 5 • Read Nehemiah 2:17–20

21. What convinced the people to build the wall of Jerusalem with Nehemiah?

22. How could a Law-and-Gospel message be patterned after Nehemiah's words? See Isaiah 1:18–20; 2:1–5.

23. What was the charge that Nehemiah's opponents laid against the Israelites in order to discourage them? What truth did they twist in order to make their accusation stick?

24. What did Nehemiah deny to the enemies of the Israelites in his response to them? Why do they have no portion or claim in Jerusalem?

Day 3 • Read Ezra 10:1–8

11. What was proposed to remedy the situation concerning illegitimate marriages among the Israelites?

12. How would you describe Ezra's manner of leadership in this issue? How did he manage to gain the cooperation of the Judean people?

13. Read 2 Corinthians 6:14–7:1. What does "unequally yoked" mean in the context of a marriage between two different faiths? Compare with Deuteronomy 22:10. How does the distinction between "clean" and "unclean" apply to Ezra's dilemma?

14. Read Matthew 22:23–33 and Romans 7:2. What is the limitation placed upon the covenant of marriage that is not found in the covenant of faith in Christ?

15. Consider divorce and the tragic breakup of many families in light of the consequences that followed King David's adultery with Bathsheba in 2 Samuel 12:15–23. Why doesn't forgiveness always remove the effects of sin?

Day 4 • Read Ezra 10:9–17

16. What was preventing the assembled Israelites from addressing the intermarriage issue that was brought before Ezra? Why couldn't they gather inside the temple building?

17. What solution was proposed as an alternative to investigating every family immediately in Jerusalem?

18. Who were the men opposed to this plan? For what reasons would you think these people would object?

19. Read Malachi 2:7–16. In what way were some people of Judah faithless regarding their marriages? Would you see Ezra's intermarriage situation differently if it were the case that the men had divorced their believing wife and married a pagan woman instead?

20. How does Ezra's particular style of leadership set a good example for church leaders today?

Day 5 • Read Ezra 10:18–44

21. How long did it take to investigate all of the unlawful marriages in Israel (vv. 16–17)?

22. In what ways does faithful and loving church discipline strengthen a congregation? What harm would it bring if it were consistently avoided? Is there ever a situation where it would be better for a brief time to set aside a matter of discipline? Why or why not?

23. Read Leviticus 6:1–7; Joshua 22:15–31; and 2 Chronicles 26:16–21. From these passages in various parts of the Old Testament, how would you describe a "breach of faith" against God in the context of life and in worship?

24. Why is it that when a leader goes astray in a church, it is more harmful than when a member of the rank and file is involved in a sinful incident?

25. Looking over what we have studied the last five weeks, compare and contrast the roles of Zerubbabel, who was engaged in building the temple, and Ezra, who was called to "build up" God's people.

Day 3 • Read Ezra 8:1–20

11. Ezra's tone changes as he now speaks as "I." Read Acts 16:10; 20:7; and John 21:23–25. What is an advantage of reporting historical events in the first person ("I", "we", etc.)? How are eyewitness reports the most reliable?

12. Ezra is careful to list first the priests and the descendant of King David (vv. 1–2). What might be the significance of this ordering?

13. The twelve family heads stand for the twelve tribes that comprise the entire Israelite nation. Based on Galatians 3:26–29 and Ephesians 2:11–16, in what way is the Christian Church a part of the true Israel?

14. Before they set out on their journey, what group of people was found to be lacking in Ezra's traveling party? Why was it necessary that they come with Ezra?

15. As mentioned in verse 20, temple servants were put to work doing jobs associated with worship, apart from the work of the Levites and priests. What were the circumstances surrounding the arrangements described in Joshua 9:3–9, 19–27; and 1 Kings 5:13–18?

Day 4 • Read Ezra 8:21–30

16. What is the purpose for the fast that Ezra declares for the people to observe before they set out on their journey to Jerusalem? What is the benefit of fasting?

17. Think about a time when travel was especially difficult or even dangerous for you. How did you see the protecting hand of the Lord through that ordeal? In what ways did it change the way you thought about His protection for your next journey?

18. Ezra felt that he could not accept a Persian armed escort, lest it be misinterpreted from his earlier words that he actually didn't believe that God would protect him. Could there have been a different way for Ezra to handle the situation?

19. Read Numbers 2:2, 17 and 3:5–10. How were the vessels for worship protected during the Israelites' journey through the wilderness under the leadership of Moses? Who were the ones entrusted with the holy items in Ezra's group?

20. Read Acts 21:27–36 and 22:22–29. How did Paul make use of military protection and his political rights?

Day 5 • Read Ezra 8:31–36

21. Compare this part of Ezra's report with the information in Ezra 7:7–9. How long did it take the group to travel approximately 900 miles to Jerusalem?

22. How does Ezra describe the attacks from enemies along the way? Whether they actually experienced ambush attempts or not, what was the real cause of their safe journey?

23. Psalm 121 is among several short psalms of praise, called Songs of Ascents, that God's people sang as they were ascending the slopes of Jerusalem's hills to arrive at the temple. With what words and phrases does this psalm confess our trust in God's protection?

24. Refer back to Ezra 8:15. What was significant about the three days of rest once Ezra and the returned exiles arrived in Jerusalem in 8:32? What do the three days bring to mind for the Christian (Matthew 12:40; 1 Corinthians 15:4)?

25. Why was it important that the temple vessels be carefully weighed, recorded, and handed over to the attending priest in Jerusalem?

10. The Small Catechism's explanation of the Ninth Commandment speaks against using a "scheme," or getting what belongs to our neighbor "in a way which only appears right." How could the letter to the king in Ezra 4 be characterized as a "way which only appears right"? What about this type of sin do you think would make it especially damaging if it were to happen to you?

Day 3 • Read Ezra 5

11. What was Tattenai's tactic that he employed, hoping further to stall the work on the Jerusalem temple?

12. What was the Judean leaders' response to their adversaries' challenge? Were they honest about the reason why the first temple was destroyed?

13. Read Haggai 1:13–2:9 and Zechariah 8:1–17. In what ways did these prophets help and support the people rebuilding the temple in Jerusalem?

14. The prophets above encouraged the people with God's Word. What do you find most encouraging when you hear God's Word?

15. The prophets preached "in the name of the God of Israel." Read Numbers 6:22–27; 1 Kings 8:26–30; and Lamentations 3:55–57. How is God's name properly used? What kind of help might someone receive from the use of His name?

Day 4 • Read Ezra 6:1–12

16. What did it mean for the builders of the temple that the decree of Cyrus was found in the royal archives?

17. According to Darius's decree, what does Tattenai and all of the other officials of the province have to do in addition to leaving the Judean people alone?

18. In your opinion, why did King Darius request prayers for himself and his sons from the Israelites? Read 1 Timothy 2:1–6. For what do we pray concerning our leaders?

19. What would be the reason for King Darius to prescribe such a violent death sentence for anyone who alters or disobeys his command?

20. Read Hebrews 12:1–3 and Galatians 3:13–14. What is the shame that Christ endured in His death? Compare His crucifixion with the punishment that Darius threatens in Ezra 6:11.

Day 5 • Read Ezra 6:13–22

21. The original order from King Darius came during the second year of his reign over Persia. How long did it take to finish the temple building after King Darius ordered the adversaries to keep away (v. 15)?

22. Read Leviticus 4:22–26. According to Ezra, what was the specified purpose for the sacrifice of the goats at the temple's dedication?

23. Read 1 Kings 12:1–20. How did King Rehoboam's actions lead to Israel's split into the Northern and Southern Kingdoms?

24. Passover was a yearly observance, but whenever its celebration is recorded in Scripture, it connects to a significant event. What is the significant historical event where the Passover is mentioned in the following verses:

Exodus 13:3–10

Joshua 5:10–12

2 Kings 23:21–23

Ezra 6:19–22

25. Read 1 Kings 8:1–11, 62–66. What were the differences between Solomon's dedication ceremony and the ceremony in Ezra? What has changed in the exiles' reaction to the new temple since they laid the foundation in Ezra 3:12?

12. Read Numbers 3:1–13. How were priests and Levites related?

13. Compare the numbers of Levites to the number of priests in Ezra 2:36–42. Now consult Numbers 26:57–62. What is the contrast that shows up in the Ezra record?

14. Why are some listed by family and others listed by city? What was the difficulty that presented itself in Ezra 2:59–63?

15. How would consulting the Urim and Thummim solve the Levitical genealogy issue? Refer to 1 Samuel 14:41.

Day 4 • Read Ezra 3:1–7; Leviticus 23:33–43

16. What activities initiated the construction of the temple in Jerusalem? Why did the altar have to be set up first?

17. The Law (Torah or "teaching") of Moses was the authority by which God's people would reinstitute His chosen form of worship. What role did the Torah play in the revival of temple worship? (Compare with the reforms recorded in 2 Kings 23:1–7.)

18. According to Leviticus 23:33–43, what was God's reason for instituting the Feast of Booths? How would this help the exiles who returned to Judea nearly a millennium after Moses?

19. Why would the people be fearful of their new neighbors as they are rededicating the altar of sacrifice in Jerusalem (Ezra 3:3)? Compare a few translations on this verse, as much as you are able.

20. Compare the names by which the people are identified in Ezra 1:1, 3, 4, 5, 11; 2:1, 70; and 3:1. What is the significance of calling them "children of Israel" once they have finally returned to their own land?

Day 5 • Read Ezra 3:8–13

21. What was the occasion for weeping when the temple's new foundation was laid? What was it about the former temple that made the older Israelites react this way?

22. Read 2 Kings 16:10–16; 18:13–16; and 21:4–15. What damage, both spiritual as well as physical, had been done to Solomon's temple prior to its complete destruction? How could that memory have contributed to the mixed reaction of sadness along with joy?

23. If you are comfortable, share an event in your life that was both joyful and sad. Does one emotion win out over the other? What about when a long time passes and you look back on it—what changes in your feelings about that episode?

24. What recurring theme do you see in Ezra 3:11 and other temple psalms? See Psalms 118; 136; and 150. God's "steadfast love," or "mercy," is described as favor rendered without an obligation to do so.

25. What hymns, psalms, and Scripture readings would you consider as appropriate for a church dedication or anniversary? What would be the general theme of your festival service?

Day 3 • Read Daniel 5

11. Who was the ruler who took over the throne of Babylon after Nebuchadnezzar (v. 1, 18)? How does this king come to know of Daniel (v. 12)?

12. What took place at the banquet that prompted the appearance of the supernatural handwriting on the wall?

13. What other warnings had been given to the Babylonian kings before King Belshazzar?

14. Compare Daniel's interpretation of the writing on the wall with Joseph's interpretation of Pharaoh's dreams in Genesis 41. Note and discuss also any difference between the two accounts.

Day 4 • Read Daniel 1; Esther 2; 4

15. Read Daniel 1. How does Daniel gain a position of privilege and influence in Babylon? Who also benefits from this opportunity?

16. Similar to Daniel's rise of influence in Babylon, what were the God-given qualities and talents in Joseph (Genesis 41:37–57) that led him to a high position in Egypt?

17. It is possible that Esther had no other choice but to be "taken" (Esther 2:8) to fulfill the king's demand for a replacement queen. In what way does God use this event for His purposes?

18. According to Esther 4:11–14, what two pieces of advice does Mordecai impress upon Esther when it comes to the idea that God acts through a person's vocation?

19. What would be the best ways for a Christian to influence society today? Why?

Day 5 • Read 2 Chronicles 36:22–23; Isaiah 45

20. What role does King Cyrus play in the Old Testament account of the Babylonian exile?

21. How does Isaiah speak of Cyrus, over two centuries before he even comes to power (Isaiah 45:4)?

22. Compare and contrast the Lord's use of Cyrus, Pharaoh (Exodus 7:1–13), and Caesar Augustus (Luke 2:1–20) in His plan for His chosen people.

23. Read Isaiah 45:15–25. How is it that God "hides Himself" (v. 15)? What is His ultimate goal for Israel and for all believers?

God also provides for us when we are overwhelmed with discouragement and depression. Look! Up ahead! Can it be? Is it a bird? a plane? Superman? Infinitely better! We have a people mover who is greater than the mighty Nehemiah. His name is Jesus.

Luke records our Lord's first sermon in his Gospel: "The Spirit of the Lord is upon Me, because He has anointed Me to proclaim good news to the poor. He has sent Me to proclaim liberty to the captives and recovering of sight to the blind, to set at liberty those who are oppressed, to proclaim the year of the Lord's favor" (4:18–19). Then he says, "Today this Scripture has been fulfilled in your hearing" (4:21). Throughout his Gospel, Luke points us to Jesus, who has come to move the lost, the least, and the last!

To a dead son in the village of Nain, He says, "Young man, I say to you, arise" (7:14). Jesus tells a woman with a flow of blood for eighteen years, "Your faith has made you well" (8:48). He lovingly says to Jairus's daughter, "Child, arise" (8:54). To starved, famished, and empty people, Christ says, "Come, for everything is now ready" (14:17). To the Romans who scourged Him, spit on Him, and spiked Him, He says over and over again, "Father, forgive them, for they know not what they do" (23:34). And to every one of us He will one day announce with a loving gleam in His eye, "Truly, I say to you, today you will be with Me in Paradise" (23:43).

Not an Airport Gate, but the Pearly Gates

Sometimes, it sure seems as though we are stuck in life's airport with no possibility of making it to our gate. It seems impossible! And left to our own devices, it would be absolutely impossible. But, thanks be to God, we have been provided with a mighty people mover in our Lord Jesus Christ.

Because we have a flight home that God will not let us miss, in Baptism Jesus moves us from a condemnation to hell to an eternity in heaven. With His own true body and blood given for us in the Lord's Supper, our Savior moves us from emptiness to fullness, from sorrow to joy. In the Absolution our pastor announces, we have been moved from death to life—a new life in Christ that is free and certain and forever!

VENGEANCE BELO

After the fall of the Northern Kingdom of Israel (also referred to as Samaria) in 722 BC, the Assyrians repopulated the area with people from all over the ancient Near East. Two times in the Book of Ezra we learn that the Assyrians relocated more people in Samaria (Ezra 4:2, 10).

Open hostility between these Samaritans and Judahites becomes evident when Zerubbabel, Jeshua, and others told the Samaritans, "You have nothing to do with us in building a house to our God; but we alone will build to the Lord, the God of Israel, as King Cyrus the king of Persia has commanded us" (Ezra 4:3). This kind of ill will shows itself in the Book of Nehemiah by means of several confrontations with Sanballat, who apparently had command over "the army of Samaria." He enlisted Tobiah the Ammonite and Geshem the Arab to be in league with him against the Judahites (Nehemiah 4:1–8). His daughter even married the high priest Eliashib's grandson, Jehoiada's son. Nehemiah's response was decisive. He drove him away (Nehemiah 13:28).

Calling Down Evil upon Them

Nehemiah's prayers regarding these enemies are shocking. "Hear, O our God, for we are despised. Turn back their taunt on their own heads and give them up to be plundered in a land where they are captives. Do not cover their guilt, and let not their sin be blotted out from Your sight, for they have provoked You to anger in the presence of the builders" (Nehemiah 4:4–5). "Remember Tobiah and Sanballat, O my God, according to these things that they did, and also the prophetess Noadiah and the rest of the prophets who wanted to make me afraid" (6:14). "Remember them, O my God, because they have desecrated the priesthood and the covenant of the priesthood and the Levites" (13:29).

Nehemiah appears to be acting harshly, even vindictively. His petitions fall in line with these prayers from the Psalms. "O God, break the teeth in their mouths" (58:6). "The righteous will rejoice when . . . he will bathe his feet in the blood of the wicked" (58:10). "Blessed shall he be who takes your little ones and dashes them against the rock!" (137:9).

The sentiments of broken teeth, bloody baths, and baby bashing are not confined to a few psalms; in fact, thirty-two of them fall under the ominous title "imprecatory," which means to call down evil upon someone. They are often categorized into these three groups, as shown in the chart.

IMPRECATORY PSALMS

Prayers Against	Psalms
Social Enemies	58, 94
National Enemies	68, 74, 79, 83, 129, 137
Personal Enemies	5, 6, 7, 9, 10, 17, 28, 31, 35, 40, 52, 54, 55, 56, 59, 69, 70, 71, 104, 109, 139, 140, 141, 143

How did such vengeful words make their way into the Bible? Are these texts really part of same the same tradition that admonishes the faithful to "love your enemies" (Matthew 5:44), turn the other cheek (Luke 6:29), walk the extra mile (Matthew 5:41), and "bless and do not curse" (Romans 12:14)?

But before we point out the failings of Nehemiah and other Old Testament believers, we have to face the fact that in the *first* book about the *Christian* Church, and this in its *first* chapter, Luke records an event when Peter quotes from both Psalms 69 and 109, two of the most notorious imprecatory psalms. The apostle goes on to quote from these prayers with the words that these texts "had to be fulfilled, *which the Holy Spirit spoke* beforehand by the mouth of David concerning Judas" (Acts 1:16, emphasis added). Does this mean that imprecatory prayers were inspired by the Holy Spirit? How did this state of affairs come about?

The answer comes in Genesis. Here the Lord promises Abra[ha]m, "I will curse him who curses you" (12:3 NKJV). When the same verbal root "to curse" appears in Israel's malediction texts, it appears in a *passive* form; for example, "Cursed be the man who makes a carved or cast metal image" (Deuteronomy 27:15). God curses in the *active* aspect ("I will curse"); Israel curses in the *passive* aspect ("cursed be"). This grammar and theology are summed up when the Lord says in Romans 12:19, "Vengeance is Mine, I will repay."

Paul makes it clear in Galatians 3:29 that the baptized "are Abraham's offspring, [and are thus] heirs according to promise." As heirs of Abraham through Christ, we are heirs of God's promises of blessing *and* cursing. It should not surprise us, therefore, that the theology of imprecation appears in many places in the New Testament. The classic example comes in Galatians 1:8–9, where the apostle invokes an eternal curse on the enemies of the Gospel. Standing in the same tradition, Jesus also uttered prayers of imprecation on His enemies (such as in Matthew 11:20–24).

Nehemiah's prayers against his enemies therefore fit within this larger biblical revelation. And, on closer inspection, we see that Nehemiah never takes the role of avenger. He leaves that up to God. Far from being vindictive, Nehemiah leaves his enemies in God's hands for judgment. The significance is that he leaves room for the Lord to demonstrate mercy to those who repent of their sins.

To be sure, love and forgiveness are always our first response to our adversaries. But what is our response to sustained violence and unthinkable acts of hatred? Martin Luther puts it this way: "We should pray that our enemies be converted and become our friends and, if not, that their doing and designing be bound to fail and have no success and that their persons perish rather than the Gospel and the kingdom of Christ" (WLS § 3517).

Armed for Battle—On to Victory

A war is going on, and it is a war of opposing powers with eternal consequences. In this war, the baptized experience casualties, traitors, and triumphs. Our weapon is the "sword of the Spirit, which is the word of God" (Ephesians 6:17). This armament is not one of sweet passivity, but of life and death. It is a weapon that includes both "the kindness and the severity of God" (Romans 11:22). In times of acute and ongoing distress, we must invoke the severity of God as expressed in imprecatory prayers.

We can do so knowing that such prayer is God's gift, so that when we are suffering, we are able to hold fast to our human dignity, while at the same time endure hardship nonviolently. For all the while we know that our prayers are heard and we will be preserved and delivered by God. Although the battle still rages, His enemies are defeated in Christ; victory is ours and will be fully enjoyed at the end. This is certain. And so, imprecatory prayer is our way of coming before the Lord and throwing the sword to Him, "the battle is the LORD's" (see 1 Samuel 17:47).

Portions of this article were adapted from "Broken Teeth, Bloody Baths, and Baby Bashing: Is There Any Place in the Church for Imprecatory Psalms?" (*Concordia Journal*, October 2006 [vol. 32, no. 4]).

He Only Has Eyes for You

The song "I Only Have Eyes for You" was composed in 1934 by Harry Warren and Al Dublin. It has been recorded by numerous musicians, including Peggy Lee, Frank Sinatra, and Art Garfunkel. The Flamingos' version of this song is ranked number 158 in Rolling Stone Magazine's list of the 500 Greatest Songs of All Time.

The Lord has His own version of this golden oldie, and it appears in the longest prayer in the Book of Nehemiah (9:5–38). The prayer delights in God's ability to see the suffering of His people when they were slaves in Egypt, while it concludes with these words: "Behold, we are slaves this day; in the land that You gave to our fathers to enjoy its fruit and its good gifts, behold, we are slaves" (9:36). The prayer is based on God's ability and willingness to see the afflictions of His people.

Fun-House Mirrors

Those praying were in the faraway Persian province of Yehud. This gigantic empire, stretching from India to Egypt, could not care less about them. Persia was distant, aloof, cold, and calculating. It looked at the Judeans as cogs in their vast and ever-growing political machine. God's people were nothing in their eyes.

When I was a child, one of our family rituals every summer was going to Elitch Gardens in Denver, Colorado. The park had all kind of rides and enough sticky cotton candy to amaze my little life. But what always fascinated me most were the fun-house mirrors. Some mirrors would make me look tall and skinny. Others would make me look short and fat. And still others would make me look ugly and creepy. None of them reflected who I really was.

And neither do the mirrors that surround us. Turn on the TV, surf the Net, go to a mall, or pick up a magazine. There we see perfect people with perfect families and perfect marriages delighting in perfect jobs. And when these images seductively summon us to gaze into their glass, what do we see? We see that we don't measure up. You name it, we don't have it. Addicted to how the world sees us, we begin feeling tall and skinny, short and fat, ugly and creepy. If we look into these mirrors long enough, we begin to languish, lose heart, and feel worthless.

And when we feel worthless, we not only discount ourselves, but we also we begin discounting everybody else. You name them; we discount them all—spouses, children, colleagues, pastors, and parents. When we feel like nothing, we treat other people like nothing. We sell each other off for cut rate prices, slashing-and-burning reputations. Obsessed witl what we don't have, we get stuck in the game of gossip, th silent stares, and the jungle of judgment.

Seeing Things Straight

Let me be as clear as possible. How you stack up in th eyes of others does not reflect who you really are. Your identit is in the Lord, and He sees your pain and you deep hurt. In His eyes, you are prized priceless, preferred, and precious. Le me explain.

Value is based o ownership. A car owned b Elvis Presley is worth a lo more than my Mazd Protegé, which our thre children have dented damaged, dinged, an almost destroyed! Valu is also determined b how much someone i willing to pay. My car i worth what someone i willing to pay for it. Which when translated, means not whole lot!

So value is based on ownershi God has created and claimed, fashione and formed us. We are His sons and Hi daughters through faith in Jesus Christ (see Galatian 3:29). And value is based on how much someone is willin to pay. Our God is willing to lay down the life of His Son jus for us.

But why trust the Lord to place value on us? Just who is H anyway? Again, let me be as clear as possible.

The prayer in Nehemiah 9 announces that the Lord i able to explain the past, predict the future, and do things i the present that are radically new. He is the holy, suprem awesome, eternal God, and there is no other! As the world Creator, He "made heaven, the heaven of heavens, with all the host, the earth and all that is on it, the seas and all that is i them" (Nehemiah 9:6). As the Redeemer, He called Abrahan gave him a covenant, brought Israel out of Egypt, gave them H Word, and provided for them in the wilderness. He defeate their enemies and brought them into a land flowing wit milk and honey. The Lord is "a God ready to forgive, graciou and merciful, slow to anger and abounding in steadfast love" (Nehemiah 9:17). And when they cried out to God, He heard and, in compassion, delivered them time after time.

Within Nehemiah 9, the prayer announces that the Lord isn't a system, a force, an idea, a movement, a doctrine, or a higher power. He is a person, and He says, "I only have eyes for you."

We Are in His Sight Always, Even Forever

Where are we valuable? Not in our eyes. When our eyes are wide open, we see our duplicity, dishonesty, idolatry, and our ongoing hypocrisy. There is nothing at all valuable for us to see. So where are we valuable?

God says, "In My eyes!" To quote Luther, "Although in supreme trials you seem nothing in your own eyes and are condemned as one cast off by the world, in My eyes you are glorious. Therefore you may be vile in your own eyes, in the eyes of the world, and even in those of your brothers. Fear not. In My eyes I regard you as a precious jewel" (AE 17:88).

But there is more.

In the baptismal flood, God claimed you as His own, and on a hill called Calvary, He paid for you with His Son, Jesus. And this means the Lord has more than just eyes for you. Oh, my! He has a heart for you. Jesus says, "As the Father has loved Me, so have I loved you" (John 15:9). The Lord has ears for you. Jesus says, "Ask, and it will be given to you; seek, and you will find; knock, and it will be opened to you" (Matthew 7:7). And He has body and blood for you. Jesus says, "This is My body, which is given for you. Do this in remembrance of Me. . . . This cup that is poured out for you is the new covenant in My blood" (Luke 22:19–20).

The slaughtered Lamb, the empty tomb, and the gift of the Holy Spirit all testify to this one indisputable fact. The Lord loves these lyrics: "The moon may be high, but I can't see a thing in the sky, 'cause I only have eyes for you."

SOUL FOOD

"You've got to taste this!" So said our mothers as they thrust lima beans into our face.

"You've got to taste this!" So say our spouses as they thrust their latest concoction of tuna casserole into our face.

But all this pales in comparison to the taste test conducted by a gourmet cook as she thrust dog food upon unsuspecting guests!

It happened at a reception near Denver. The dog food was served on delicate little crackers with a wedge of imported cheese, bacon chips, an olive, and a sliver of pimento on top. It was hors d'oeuvres à la Alpo! The hostess had just completed a gourmet cooking course and decided it was time to put her skills to the ultimate test. After doctoring up those miserable morsels and putting them on a couple of silver trays, with a sly grin she watched them all disappear.

Ezra and Nehemiah know what it is like to eat not food, but God's Word. They are in the tradition of believers who not only read and study Holy Scripture but also internalize it. Jeremiah says that when God's words came, he ate them (Jeremiah 15:16). Ezekiel (Ezekiel 2:8–3:3) and John (Revelation 10:9–10) likewise consume the Word of the Lord. The metaphor of eating the Bible implies that reading it is more than defining its words and locating its people and places. God gives His Word not only to inform, but also, all the more, to nourish and strengthen us.

and the oxen; and poured
money, and overthrew the table
said unto them that sold doves,
his disciples remembered that it
The zeal of thine house hath

Consuming and Digesting the Word

Holy Scripture plays a huge part in the Books of Ezra and Nehemiah. Together, they refer to Scripture twenty-nine times, twenty-eight of which are references to the Pentateuch (that is, the first five books of the Old Testament). Because this Word is *written* on a scroll, it is enduring. Holy Writ is our permanent source of truth, power, and light. It guides Jerusalem's community to offer acceptable sacrifices (Ezra 3:2), regulate ministries (Ezra 6:18), live faithfully (Nehemiah 8:8), and repent of their sins (Ezra 9:10–15). God's living Word brings great joy. This is why Judahites publicly read and studied it (Ezra 7:10).

To empower us, God places His Word into our lives and mouths as well. His Word is "the power of God for salvation to everyone who believes" (Romans 1:16). The psalmist celebrates that it is "a lamp to my feet and a light to my path" (Psalm 119:105). God's Word "is living and active, sharper than any two-edged sword" (Hebrews 4:12).

But isn't there something tastier, more appetizing, with a bit more pizzazz? Here it is. For breakfast: one-half grapefruit, one piece of whole wheat toast (no butter), eight ounces of skim milk, and black coffee. For lunch: four ounces of lean broiled chicken breast (skin removed), one cup of steamed zucchini, herbal tea (no sugar), one Oreo cookie. For a snack: the rest of the package of Oreo cookies, one quart chocolate almond ice cream, one jar of hot fudge. For dinner, the menu calls for two loaves of garlic bread (heavy on the butter), one large sausage and pepperoni pizza (extra cheese), a large milk shake with whipped cream. And for dessert: three Milky Way candy bars and an entire frozen cheesecake!

Oh, we try to stay on a spiritual diet of God's Word, which brings vigor and health and strength and power. But then we slip—one Oreo cookie. We lurch for one crumb of coveting one piece of porn, one slice of slander, one sip of sarcasm, and then the rest of the package of Oreo cookies! We just can't get enough, and it is killing us!

Satan, our enemy, thrusts this junk food before us on silver trays. With a sly grin, he watches it all disappear. Filled to the

brim with his miserable morsels, our desire to regularly study, memorize, learn, understand, defend, trust, believe, love, and live out this Word of God becomes a chore, a bore, a snore, until we say, "No more!"

This is why the Lord serves up one more Word. This Word became flesh and dwelt among us, full of grace and truth. His appetite is defined in Hebrews 2:9: "So that by the grace of God He might taste death for everyone."

Talk about a taste test! This was it for all time! Jesus tasted the demonic delight called death: the soldiers' spit and their cheap wine. Our Lord tasted sweat running down His cheeks and His very own blood. But there was more. Jesus drank the cup of the Father's wrath to the very last drop. It killed Him.

Jesus not only tasted death—He swallowed him up, chewed him up, and spit him out! "Death is swallowed up in victory" (1 Corinthians 15:54).

And now the Spirit of the risen Christ creates in us a new hunger and a new thirst for His Word. Spirit-led, "like newborn babes, [we] long for the pure spiritual milk . . . [now that we] have tasted that the Lord is good" (1 Peter 2:2–3). We long to hear, read, mark, learn, and inwardly digest this precious Word.

The Heavenly Diet

The tasks before us, like those in front of Ezra and Nehemiah, are urgent. There is a world to evangelize, a Church to love, and a host of righteous causes to fight for. And we live in an age when the authority of the Bible has been replaced by the authority of the self. We so desperately need that spiritual nourishment of God's Word, yet there seem to be so many obstacles in our way—so many temptations to get on another diet. Yet the nourishment He gives us in His Word preserves and sustains us even in the face of those temptations.

When we are on a steady diet of Holy Writ and the devil accuses us, we say, "There is therefore now no condemnation for those who are in Christ Jesus" (Romans 8:1). This food enlivens hope in the midst of our hopelessness: "According to His great mercy, He has caused us to be born again to a living hope" (1 Peter 1:3). When enemies mock and deny the Bible, we have a more powerful Word. Jesus pledges, "Heaven and earth will pass away, but My words will not pass away" (Matthew 24:35). May God grant that we take His Word and read, mark, learn, and inwardly digest it all the days of our lives!

Clearing Up the Confusion

The first time the term "Jew" (the Hebrew word is *Yehudim*) appears in the Bible is in the Books completed after the exile, such as Ezra and Nehemiah. It occurs several times in both books. However, a better translation of *Yehudim*, which is rendered in most English versions as "Jew," would be "Judahite." The Persian province of Yehud (that is, the territory of Judah) consisted of Judahites, not Jews. The beliefs and practices of these post-exilic believers must be distinguished from what later developed into Judaism from around 200 BC.

Why is this analysis important?

©Steven Allan/iStockphoto.com

A chief component of a belief system technically referred to as "premillennial dispensationalism" is that Ezra and Nehemiah are stellar examples of the belief that the Jews of today have direct links to God's promises to Israel in the Old Testament. You may have come upon this kind of thinking before. The idea was made popular some years ago by the Left Behind books written by Tim LaHaye and Jerry B. Jenkins. One of the principal themes running through those books is this notion that modern-day Jews receive the eternal blessings that God promised to Old Testament Israel.

This is a grave misunderstanding!

So, What's in a Name?

The Left Behind series understands the following terms as synonymous: Israelite, Hebrew, Jew, and Israeli. In their literature, LaHaye and Jenkins make statements such as these: "God promised the land to the Jews when they came out of Egypt." Or, "Beginning with Abraham, the Lord promises to bless the Israelis forever."

However, biblically, theologically, and historically, the four terms of Israelite, Hebrew, Jew, and Israeli have different definitions. Unpacking the terms, while a somewhat challenging and complex task, yields important interpretive insights.

First, an *Israelite* is an Old Testament believer in Yahweh, the God who revealed Himself to Abraham, Isaac, and Jacob, and who in subsequent historical events confirmed His promise to send the Seed (Christ), who would crush the serpent's head (Genesis 3:15).

Second, the term *Hebrew* is often used in the Old Testament when Israelites are in a pagan environment. For instance, in Genesis, Joseph is described as a Hebrew by both Potiphar's wife (39:17) and Pharaoh's servants (41:12), and Jonah describes himself as a Hebrew to the sailors on the boat (Jonah 1:9). To this extent, the terms *Israelite* and *Hebrew* are synonymous in the Old Testament. These believing Israelites (or Hebrews) are the spiritual forefathers of all who confess that Jesus Christ is Lord (Romans 4:12, 16).

Third, the term *Jew*, however, is more complex, because the word has both racial and religious connotations. For instance, some consider themselves to be both Jewish by race and Christian by faith. These people sometimes refer to themselves as "Messianic Jews" who embrace Jewish ethnicity along with faith in Jesus Christ.

Whereas the term *Jew* can identify one's race or ethnicity, it may also define someone who is an adherent of the religion called "Judaism," which is distinct from the Christ-centered faith of the Old Testament. Adherents of Judaism profess allegiance to the Old Testament, but they also embrace the Mishnah, Talmud, and other ancient rabbinic writings. Belief in these documents promotes an interpretation of the Old Testament that is not consistent with the Christ-centered, grace-based teaching of the New Testament. Modern-day Judaism varies widely in religious commitments and beliefs; several of the more prominent branches of this religion are Hasidic, Orthodox, Conservative, and Reformed.

Fourth, an *Israeli* is a citizen of the state of Israel, established in 1948, who may or may not identify with the religion of Judaism.

It is therefore accurate to speak of certain people who are alive today as Jews and Israelis. On the other hand, it is inaccurate to say that there are any Israelites or Hebrews living today. Yet this inaccuracy pervades the writings of Left Behind, and by failing to make this distinction, the authors identify modern-day Jews and Israelis as the Old Testament recipients of God's promises. However, the Bible teaches that the promises made to Israelites and Hebrews in the Old Testament find their fulfillment not with Jews or Israelis, but rather with Christ and His Church.

In God's plan of salvation, there is no difference between Jew and Gentile, Israel and the Church

Christ's Church: The New Testament Israel

Therefore, in contrast to the theology of Left Behind, in the present age God does not have two different plans, one for Jews and one for the Church. Rather, the New Testament consistently speaks of one true vine, one foundation, one way, or one olive tree. All of these are symbols portraying the unity within the one elect people of God, made up of both Jews and Gentiles, who by faith are thereby declared to be children of Abraham, who is "the father of all who believe" (Romans 4:11). Paul uses the similar analogies of "one new man" (Ephesians 2:15) and "fellow heirs, members of the same body" (Ephesians 3:6) to emphasize that God has taken these two peoples and made them one in Christ. John the Baptist indicated, "And do not begin to say to yourselves, 'We have Abraham as our father.' For I tell you, God is able from these stones to raise up children for Abraham" (Luke 3:8). From a New Testament perspective, the true descendants of Abraham are not present-day Jews o Israelis, but rather believers in Jesus. "And if you are Christ's then you are Abraham's offspring, heirs according to promise (Galatians 3:29).

The inheritance promises that God gave to Abrahan were made effective through Christ, Abraham's true Seed. Al spiritual benefits are derived from Jesus, and apart from Hin there is no participation in the promises made to Abrahan (Galatians 3:26–29). Since Jesus is the fulfillment of th covenant made to Abraham, all who bless Him and His peopl will be blessed, and all who curse Him and His people will b cursed (Genesis 12:3; Galatians 3:7–8). These promises are no directed toward any particular ethnic group. Th Church, and not Jews or Israelis, is the tru Israel of God (Romans 2:28–29).

According to Scriptur salvation is neither earned no deserved, nor is it based o ethnic descent or natural birth Apart from Christ, there is n special divine favor on an member of any ethnic grou In privileging ethnic Jews c modern Israelis with a distin plan of salvation, the Left Behin books obscure this central teachin of the Bible.

Fulfilled in Christ

The Bible does not support the teaching that Go has a special plan for bringing Jews to faith in Christ. Th is because in God's plan of salvation, there is no differen between Jew and Gentile, Israel and the Church. Rather tha teaching that these are two separate communities with tw different futures, the Scriptures testify to a continuity betwee the old and new covenants, and thus to a continuity betwee Israel and the Church.

Put another way, Old Testament Israel is a precursor for th Church, for it is prophesied in the Old Testament that God redemptive purposes include Gentiles. Therefore, the Churc is not an interruption in the redemptive plan of God, b rather the fulfillment of His eternal purposes. Translating th Hebrew word *Yehudim* "Judahite" and not "Jew" in the Boo of Ezra and Nehemiah is one way to clear up the confusion.

Portions of this article were adapted from *A Lutheran Response to the "Left Behind" Series*, CTCR Report, April 2004.